The Stranger's Handbook to Chester and Its E...

Thomas Hughes

Alpha Editions

This edition published in 2024

ISBN : 9789362997494

Design and Setting By
Alpha Editions
www.alphaedis.com
Email - info@alphaedis.com

As per information held with us this book is in Public Domain.
This book is a reproduction of an important historical work. Alpha Editions uses the best technology to reproduce historical work in the same manner it was first published to preserve its original nature. Any marks or number seen are left intentionally to preserve its true form.

Contents

CHAPTER I. ....- 1 -

CHAPTER II. ....- 9 -

CHAPTER III. ....- 15 -

CHAPTER IV. ....- 26 -

CHAPTER V. ....- 36 -

CHAPTER VI. ....- 46 -

CHAPTER VII. ....- 54 -

CHAPTER VIII. ....- 67 -

CHAPTER IX. ....- 81 -

CHAPTER X. ....- 90 -

CHAPTER XI. ....- 101 -

CHAPTER I.

Introduction.—The City of Chester under the Britons.—Chester a Roman Colony.—The City a prey to the Danes and Saxons.—Ethelfleda the Amazon.—Chester under the Romans.—The Palatinate Earldom.—Royal Visits to Chester.—The Plague.—The Siege of Chester.

"RARE old city of CHESTER!" writes Albert Smith in his "Struggles and Adventures of Christopher Tadpole,"—"Rare old city of Chester! Even in these days of rocket-like travelling, a man might fly all over Great Britain and Ireland, with an extra 'day ticket' for Berwick-upon-Tweed, before he saw anything half so fine as the mouldering old walls and towers of that venerable city, or looked upon anything half so fair as the prospect of vale and mountain, wooded headland, and spire-pointed plain, that surrounds it." Well said, friend Albert;—echoed, too, far and wide, by the thousands of visitors who are annually led to seek entertainment within its Walls!

Situate on the northern banks of the River Dee, the deified stream of the Ancient Britons,—built upon, or, as we ought rather to say, built *into* the solid rock, for the principal streets within the Walls are almost wholly excavations of several feet in depth—the city of Chester stands forth before the world certainly the most curious city in the British Isles, second to none of its fellows in martial strength or historic importance, and as a faithful and enduring relic of the past, "peerless and alone!"

First a settlement of the Ancient Britons—then a colony of imperial Rome—afterwards a favourite city and frequent resort of the Anglo-Saxon monarchs—now the camp and court of Hugh Lupus the Norman, nephew of the Conqueror—then the key to the subjugation of Wales, and to its union with the English crown—ever a city of loyalty and renown,—no admirer of the curious and remarkable, none who seek after the ancient and honourable, should fail to visit and explore the beauties of "rare old Chester." The eye of the stranger, be he Englishman or foreigner, European or American, will here find an ample and luxuriant field for admiration: the man of taste, who may linger within its Walls, will not depart ungratified; nor will the antiquary search here in vain for some rich and profitable treasures of investigation: in short, such is the antiquity, the peculiarity of Chester, that the stranger who can pass through without bestowing on it some little share of attention, must have a dull and incurious eye indeed.

Before we proceed to point out to the visitor the numerous objects of interest within the city, we must conform to the fashion prevalent in such matters, and, tedious though it may seem, preface our description with a condensed sketch of the

HISTORY OF CHESTER,

Some historians there are who, dealing largely in the marvellous, have attributed to Chester an existence almost coeval with the Flood. Sir Thomas Elyot, for instance, writing about 1520, gravely asserts that the name of the city was originally Neomagus, and so called from its founder Magus, the grandson of Japhet, the son of Noah, who first planted inhabitants in these islands! Were this statement authenticated, Chester would hold the dignified position of the oldest city in the universe; but, credulous as we undoubtedly are on some points, we confess to a modicum of infidelity upon this. It may have been, and from its commanding position doubtless was, one of the earliest settlements of the aboriginal inhabitants, Ancient Britons or otherwise; but farther than this, no historian, desiring to be accurate, can safely go.

Ranulph Higden, a shorn monk of Chester Abbey, attributes to the city a British foundation, namely, from Lleon Gawr, the vanquisher of the Picts, a giant of mammoth size and stature, who built a city here, chiefly *underground*, hewn out of the rock, and after a rude and disordered fashion. But let the "barefooted friar" speak for himself, from Wynkyn de Worde's edition of his Chronicle, published A.D. 1495:—

> "The Cyte of Legyons, that is Chestre, in the marches of Englonde, towarde Wales, betwegne two armes of the see, that bee named *Dee* and *Mersee*. Thys cyte in tyme of Britons, was hede and chyefe cyte of all Venedocia, that is, North Wales. Thys cyte in Brytyshe speche bete Carthleon, Chestre in Englyshe, and Cyte of Legyons also. For there laye a wynter the legyons that Julius Cezar sent for to wyne Irlonde. And after, Claudius Cezar sent legyons out of the cyte for to wynn the Islands that be called Orcades. Thys cyte hath plente of lyveland, of corn, of fleshe, and specyally of samon. Thys cyte receyveth grate marchandyse, and sendeth out also. Northumbres destroyed thys cyte sometyme, but Elfreda, lady of Mercia, bylded it agayn, and made it mouch more.
>
> "In thys cyte ben ways under erth, with vowtes and stone werke, wonderfully wrought, three chambred werkes, grete stones ingrave with old mannes names there in. Thys is that cyte that Ethelfrede, Kyng of Northumberlonde, destroyed, and sloughe there fast by nygh two thousonde monks of the mynster of Bangor. Thys is the cyte that

Kyng Edgar cam to, some tyme, with seven Kyngs that were subject to hym."

The delectable style of building above described is also thus commented upon in that poetical curiosity, the "Lyfe of St. Werburgh," by Henry Bradshaw, another monk of Chester Abbey, who flourished in sackcloth and ashes sometime previous to 1500:—

> The founder of Chester, as saith Polychronicon,
> Was Leon Gauer, a mighty strong giant;
> Which builded caves and dungeons many a one,
> No goodly buildings, ne proper, ne pleasant.
> But King Leil, a Briton sure and valiant,
> Was founder of Chester by pleasant building,
> And of Caerleil also named by the King.

Among the ancient Britons, the city was known from time immemorial as Caerlleon Vawr, and Caerlleon ar Dyfyrdwy, and was certainly with them a city of great importance, long before the advent of the Roman invaders to these shores. Equally certain is it that our primitive forefathers, unable to stem the onward current of the victorious Romans, fled in disorder from the city of Caerlleon (Chester), to the mountain fastnesses of Wales, and there concentrating themselves, defied for many a long and eventful century alike the wiles and encroachments of their enemies.

Chester, resigned to the tender mercies of the conquerors, rapidly lost its first estate;—rising again, however, under the shade of the imperial eagles, like a phœnix from its ashes, to be the chosen camp and colony of the Twentieth Legion of Cæsar. Stirring times were these for old Chester; the rude huts of the Britons, the temples and altars of the ancient Druids, the mud walls and other defences of her former possessors, all vanished like a dream, while in their place arose the proud Prætorium, the pagan temples, the stately columns, the peerless masonry, the noble statues, the massive Walls, and all the other elements of civilisation which usually followed in the wake of proud old Rome! Perhaps of the many Roman settlements in Britain, none have retained to our own time so many enduring proofs of their energetic rule as Chester. Surrounded by Walls, which for almost their entire length rest upon Roman foundations,—nay, which still exhibit to the naked eye of truth and time the evident impress of their mechanical genius,—we fancy, while we look thereon, that we see the sturdy warriors pacing to and fro, keeping watch against the enemy; while, within the city, the soldiers and inhabitants are plying the pickaxe, trowel, and spade,—here piling stone upon stone in the erection of a forum, and there planning and building the tesselated floors, the baths, and the sudatories of domestic life. Eighteen hundred years have rolled away since Julius Agricola and his

Legion held sway over the city, and yet ever since then, notwithstanding that *they* have long lain in the dust, scarce a year has passed without the encroachments of the builder, or the researches of the antiquary, bringing to light some long hidden, but valuable relic of this extraordinary people. Time and space alike forbid us to give anything like a summary of the records existing, under our very eyes, of Rome's sojourn within these walls. Other and more antiquated guide-books have long ago exhausted and worn out these topics of interest, as well as the miserable woodcuts that illustrated them; it only remains therefore for us, in the body of our work, to enumerate a few of the more prominent and accessible of these remains.

But another epoch was now rapidly dawning upon the world. Rome had passed the meridian of her splendour, and she who, so short a time before, was acknowledged mistress of the world, felt the tide of conquest and prosperity visibly ebbing away. Insurrections abroad, divisions, tumults, and murders at home, served but to aggravate and complete her fall. After the departure of the Romans from this island, Chester appears to have been alternately possessed by the Britons, the Saxons, and the Danes; by the latter, however, it was held but a very short period, being restored to the Saxons by the valiant daughter of Alfred the Great, Ethelfleda, the wife of Ethelred, Prince of Mercia. This lady is said to have repaired the city and rebuilt the walls in 907, and, as some affirm, considerably added to their former extent. After her death, the city again fell into the hands of the British princes, from whom it was recovered in 924 by King Egbert, whose death almost immediately followed this event. National affairs were then conducted according to that

> good old-fashioned plan,
> That they shall take who have the power,
> And they shall keep who can.

From this period to the Conquest, Chester has nothing of a tale to tell; but on the accession of William the Conqueror, he created his nephew Hugh Lupus, Earl of Chester, at the same time investing him with supreme authority throughout the county and city, so that he held as absolute a regal sway within those limits as the king himself had in his dominions. For one hundred and sixty years did Hugh Lupus and his successors, the seven Norman Earls of Chester, exercise their petty sovereignty over the city and county, until the death of Earl John Scot, in 1237, when Henry III. took the earldom, with all the powers annexed to it, into his own hands; and from that period to the present it has been held by the English Crown. The title of Earl of Chester was conferred by Henry upon his eldest son, afterwards Edward I. It has ever since been vested in the reigning monarch's eldest son, and is now enjoyed by his Royal Highness, Albert, Prince of Wales, the hopeful heir of our beloved Queen.

"In 1255, the Welsh, under their Prince, Llewellyn, made an irruption into this neighbourhood, carrying fire and sword to the very gates of the city. The following year Prince Edward, who had recently been created Earl of Chester, paid a visit to the city, and received the homage of the nobles of Cheshire and part of Wales." The hostile inroads of Llewellyn remained unrevenged until King Henry, in 1257, summoned his nobility and bishops to attend with their vassals at Chester, in order to invade the Principality.

"In 1272, Edward I. ascended the throne, and soon gave indications of his determination to subject Wales to the English crown. This monarch was at Chester in 1276 and 1277; in the former year he came for the purpose of summoning Llewellyn, Prince of Wales, to do him homage; who having refused to comply, he returned the next year with an army, and marching from Chester, took Rhuddlan castle, and made it a strong fortress. In 1282, we again find Edward I. in the city, where he resided from the 6th of June to the 4th of July. The following year, having been victorious in his expedition against the Welsh, he was at Chester with his Queen, and attended mass in St. Werburgh's Church, on which occasion he presented the Abbey with a cloth of great value. In September, 1284, the King was at Chester for four days, and again passed through the city in 1294, on his march to Wales, to suppress the rebellion of Madoc.

"In 1312, Edward II. came to Chester to meet Piers de Gaveston, on his return from Ireland.

"In 1399, Henry of Lancaster, in arms against Richard II., mustered his troops under the Walls of Chester, whence, on the 19th of August, he marched for Flint, and returned on the following day with Richard, whom he lodged in a tower over the outer gateway of the castle, opposite to Glover's Stone, from whence he was conveyed prisoner to London.

"In 1459, Henry VI., with Queen Margaret and her son Edward, visited Chester, and bestowed little silver swans on the Cheshire gentlemen who espoused her cause.

"On the 13th of July, 1494, Henry VII., with his mother and the Queen, came to Chester with a great retinue, from whence they proceeded to Hawarden; the Earl of Derby, and a number of 'Chester gallants' attending.

"The summer of the year 1507, was memorable here from the awful visitation of the 'sweating sickness,' which raged for a short time with great violence. It is recorded that 91 householders were carried off in three days by this distemper; but it is worthy of remark, that the female sex were generally exempt from the plague, only four having fallen victims to the disease. Cats and women have each nine lives! In 1517, the sweating sickness again proved fatal to many of the inhabitants; and the city was also infected with the plague, probably to a more serious extent. It is recorded that 'many died and others fled out of the city, insomuch that the streets were full of grass;' and 'that for want of trading the grass did grow a foot high at the Cross, and in other streets of the city.' In 1550 the city suffered severely from the sweating sickness, and to this affliction was added a great scarcity of provisions; corn selling in Chester at sixteen shillings a bushel. From the year 1602 to 1605, with few intermissions, the dreadful effects of the plague were experienced in the city. It is stated to have begun in the month of September, in the former year, at the house of one Glover, in St. John's lane, in whose house alone seven persons died. The contagion was particularly fatal in 1603 and 1604; 650 persons died in the former year, and 986 in the latter; at one period 55 died weekly.—During this dreadful visitation, the fairs of the city were suspended, the court of exchequer was removed to Tarvin, and the county assizes were held at Nantwich. The plague had abated in the month of February 1605."

From this time to 1642 no event of any great importance appears to have transpired. In the autumn of that year, however, the Cestrians found themselves embroiled in the civil war which then broke out in England; and as this was one of the proudest and most memorable epochs in our city's history, a condensed sketch of the part she and her sons played therein may not be uninteresting.

On the 25th of August, 1642, the commons being then in open rebellion against his majesty, King Charles hoisted his standard at Nottingham, and proclaimed war between himself and the parliament. "Three weeks after this, the king came to Chester, accompanied by a numerous train: the incorporated companies of the city received him and conducted him to the Pentice, where he and his suite were entertained. After the banquet, 200*l.* were presented to his majesty, and half that sum to the Prince of Wales. On the 28th of September, the king proceeded to Wrexham, escorted by the corporation to the city boundary.

"War being declared, Chester was deemed a place of great importance; and his majesty sent hither Sir Nicholas Byron, with a commission as Colonel-General of Cheshire, and Governor of Chester. A levy of 300 men was ordered by the citizens, independent of the trained bands, and a rate was made for their maintenance. The outworks and entrenchments were carried on with such vigour, that in the beginning of the summer, 1643, the *mud walls*, *mounts*, *bastions*, &c. were all completed, and several effective batteries planted."

Upon Thursday, the 19th of July, 1643, Sir William Brereton, general of the parliamentary forces, made an assault upon the works, but they were so resolutely defended, that he was beaten off, and forced to retire. On the

11th of November, the town and castle of Hawarden was surrendered to Sir William Brereton, who sent a summons to Chester, requiring the surrender of the city under pain of condign punishment in case of refusal. Governor Byron sent him for answer, that he was not to be terrified by words, but bade him "come and win the city, if he would have it." The authorities busied themselves in perfecting the defences of the city: three troops of horse were raised, for the maintenance of which the citizens assessed themselves according to their abilities, and converted 100*l.* worth of the city plate into coin, some of which pieces, stamped with the city arms, still exist in the cabinets of numismatists.

On the 13th of February, 1644, a battle was fought near Boughton, in which the enemy were forced to retire. About 100 of the royalists, chiefly Chester men, fell in this engagement.

On the 19th of September, the parliamentary forces from Beeston Castle advanced to Chester, and immediately transmitted a peremptory summons. Ere an answer could be returned, the enemy made a brisk attack upon the city, but were repulsed with loss: the city walls now constituted the only defence of the besieged. After various skirmishes on each side, the besieging commanders opened a correspondence, which, however, terminated without leading to any result.

"By the end of February, 1645, the enemy had succeeded in surrounding the city, and placed garrisons at Hoole, Rowton, Eccleston, Iron-bridge, Upton, &c. In this position affairs remained until the middle of September, when the garrison were gladdened by the news that the king was on his march for the relief of the city. The exultation of the citizens was beyond all bounds: but there is reason to believe, that in their excess of joy, measures of prudence were grievously neglected.

"On the 27th of September, his majesty, with his guards, and Lord Gerard, with the remainder of the horse, marched into the city, amidst the acclamations of the soldiers and citizens. The condition of the garrison now presented a promising appearance. Sir Marmaduke Langdale, as previously arranged, passed the river at Holt, and marching in the direction of Chester, drew up his forces upon Rowton Heath, about two miles from the city, where, on the afternoon of the same day, the decisive battle took place; the parliamentary forces, under Major-General Poyntz, totally routing the royalists. His majesty, attended by Sir Francis Gamull, and Alderman Cowper, had the mortification to witness the rout of his army from the leads of the Phœnix tower. On the following day the royal fugitive took his departure for Denbigh Castle."

On the 29th of September, the besiegers effected a breach near the Newgate, and at night made an assault, but were repulsed. On October

7th, the city was surrounded by their horse, and a violent assault made in several places. For a long time the conflict was doubtful; at length the assailants, having gained the top of the Walls, were again beaten off, thrown down, and killed. From this time the parliamentary commander despaired of taking the city by assault, and immediately converted the siege into a close blockade—a high compliment to the gallantry of the inhabitants of Chester.

"The beginning of 1646 found the garrison in want of the common necessaries of life, being so reduced as to be compelled to feed upon horses, dogs, and cats. In this extremity the garrison rejected nine different summonses, nor, till they received assurances that there was no hope of succour, did they answer the tenth. The negotiations occupied six days, when conditions were agreed to—that the garrison should march out with the honours of war, and that all the ammunition, stores, &c. in the castle, be delivered up without injury to the besieging army.

"In conformity with these articles, the brave and loyal city of Chester, which had held out twenty weeks beyond expectation, being reduced by famine to the utmost extremity, was, upon the 3rd of February, 1646, surrendered up to the parliamentary forces. For two years, nothing had been heard but the sound of warlike preparations, and during most of that time the citizens were inclosed within their Walls, the victims of starvation and constant apprehension. The incessant drains upon their property for the maintenance of the garrison, and the support of their fugitive prince, had levelled the different classes of the community to one common condition of beggary. The whole suburbs presented an undistinguishable mass of ruins, while the Walls and edifices within the city were defaced or battered down by the destructive cannon. In addition to this, the city lands were all mortgaged, the funds quite exhausted, the plate melted down, and the churches, particularly St. John's, being so long in possession of the enemy, greatly damaged."

From this eventful period down to the present day, saving a few royal visits, no circumstance has occurred of sufficient import to deserve especial mention here. So now, kind reader, having in our own way, and as briefly and modestly as possible, told our historic tale, we will close the present chapter, and in our next be ready to accompany you in your wanderings about the city.

CHAPTER II.

The Railway Station.—Chester the Terminus of Six Railways.—Flookersbrook.—Lead Works.—Canal and Bridge.—William Penn the Quaker.—Foregate Street and Old Watling Street.—Post Office and Old Bank.—The Eastgate, Roman and Mediæval.—The Eastgate of to-day.

PRESUMING, gentle reader, you have sagaciously chosen *us* as your companion, we will evince our desire to be friendly and agreeable by meeting you at the Station (for doubtless you have only just arrived by train), and taking you affectionately under our wing, will straightway introduce you to the chief Lions of Chester.

What think you, in the first place, of our noble STATION, with its elegant iron roof of sixty feet span, and its thirteen miles of railway line? Twenty years ago, the ground it stands upon, and indeed the neighbourhood around, were but plain kitchen-gardens and uninteresting fields. But a marvellous change has been effected since then, and, as if by enchantment, suburban Flookersbrook has now become the very life's-blood of the city. Stretching away on either side of us, as far as the eye can reach, we see the passengers' arrival and departure sheds, booking offices, refreshment rooms, goods and carriage depots, waterworks, gasworks, and all the other facilities and conveniences which are the usual characteristics of the railway system; while beyond the limits of the Station, and indeed of the city itself, which here intrenches upon the township of Hoole, the busy hum of life is ceaselessly heard spreading itself in every direction, and rapidly transforming the region of the plough into the turmoil of the town.

This Station is the grand central terminus of six several lines or branches, all meeting at Chester, viz., the London and North Western; the Great Western; the Birkenhead, Lancashire, and Cheshire Junction; the latter company's branch to Manchester; the Chester and Holyhead; and the Chester and Mold Railways. It was erected in 1847–8 at the joint expense of the four principal companies, and is acknowledged to be one of the handsomest, as it is certainly one of the most extensive railway establishments in the kingdom. The building was designed by C. H. Wild, Esq., C.E., and Mr. Thompson, of London (the latter the architect of the Derby station) and was built by that enterprising and well-known contractor, Mr. Thos. Brassey, whom Cheshire proudly claims as her son. The passengers' shed occupies a space of ground nearly a quarter of a mile in length, and presents to the city an elegant façade 1010 feet long, and a frontage, including the house and carriage landings, of 1160 feet. It is built of dark red fire bricks, relieved with copings and facings of Stourton stone.

At each end of the Station, and projecting from the main building, there is a shed for cabs and omnibuses awaiting the arrival of trains, each 290 feet long by 24 feet broad, covered with an iron roof.

On the inner side of the building is the General Departure Platform, extending 1010 feet in length by twenty feet in width; this and three lines of rails are covered with an exceedingly chaste and elegant iron roof of sixty feet span, designed and carried out by Mr. Wild, C.E. Behind this shed again, but visible from the general platform through the arches, is the spare carriage shed, 600 feet long by fifty-two feet broad. The whole arrangements of the buildings are admirably adapted to carry on with comfort to the public and with facility to the employés, the immense business that has so suddenly been brought to the city by the convergence of so many railways at this point.

Some idea may be formed of the extent of the business here transacted, when it is stated that of passenger trains only, there now arrive and depart upwards of ninety-eight, averaging 3500 passengers daily, or one and a quarter millions annually.

The full extent of the passengers' station from the carriage landing at the east end to the one at the west end, is 1160 feet. This noble building is an object of considerable attraction: it occupies a space of ground a quarter of a mile in length;—only half the building appears in our illustration. Great expedition was displayed by Mr. Brassey in its erection, for although the first stone was only laid in August 1847, on the 1st of August 1848 it was publicly opened for traffic.

The centre of the building, which is two stories in height, contains in the upper compartments, offices for the General Station Committee for the Chester and Holyhead, and the Great Western Railways; while on the ground floor, besides the usual offices and waiting rooms, we find the noble range of REFRESHMENT ROOMS, presided over with efficient zeal and attention by MR. HOBDAY, and his select corps of experienced assistants. If after your late journey, you feel any of the cravings of the inner man,—if dinner *à-la-mode* lie uppermost in your thoughts—if you would enjoy an invigorating cup of coffee, unimpeachable pastry, a good glass of ale, or a fragrant cigar, take a turn in the REFRESHMENT ROOMS, and the utmost wish of your soul will be incontinently gratified.

The entire number of hands employed upon the passenger station is 109, and in the goods department 130, including clerks, porters, pointsmen, &c. Between seventy and eighty goods trains arrive and depart every twenty-four hours, averaging 1600 wagons daily. In 1855, somewhere about 684,000 tons of goods, minerals and livestock passed under the manipulation of Mr. H. Parker, general goods manager. The Station Committee manufacture their own gas, the consumption of which upon this station is about 6,500,000 feet per annum. The present gas and waterworks now need to be removed more to the south-east in order to afford additional station room—the *smallness* of the present immense building being a source of *continual and growing* inconvenience. [13]

Brook Street, and Liverpool Arms Hotel.

Leaving now the Station, we see upon our left hand the lofty SHOT TOWER and LEAD WORKS of Messrs. Walker, Parker and Co., proprietors of a similar establishment near London Bridge; while on the right our view is obstructed by the handsome and commodious Bridge which here stretches across the railway, and connects the city with its suburb, Flookersbrook. Those carpetbags and cloaks, by-the-bye, however useful they may be in their way, are but superfluous companions for a jaunt about the city.

Suppose, then, we drop in at the LIVER, a most respectable HOTEL, within hail of the Station, and there depositing our luggage in one of the cosy bedrooms of that establishment, we will sally forth on our mission. After one night's sojourn at this house you'll know *your*, hotel, we promise you, for all future time. Wending our way into the city, along Brook Street, we come in due course to COWLANE BRIDGE, erected in 1776, when the canal which flows beneath it was originally projected.

Chester Cathedral, from Cowlane Bridge.

From this point we have our first glimpse of the CATHEDRAL and CITY WALLS, and a venerable sight it is, as our little illustration sufficiently testifies. Towering aloft above surrounding objects the sacred fane of St. Werburgh, presents itself to our view, in all its massive but rugged proportions, as the mother church of a vast and populous diocese. Of the Cathedral itself, as also of the Walls, we shall have abundance to say by-and-bye.

Cast your eye to the right, along the hue of the City Walls, and at their north-east angle take a distant view of yon reverend turret, overhanging the Canal. How forcibly does it remind us that—

> The days of old, though time has reft
>   The splendours they once cast,
> Yet many a relic still is left
>   To shadow forth the past!

People call it, in these days, the PHŒNIX TOWER; but two hundred years ago, and even then it was accounted *old*, the name it usually bore was *Newton's Tower*. On its lofty ramparts, in 1645, stood the royal martyr, King Charles, to witness a sanguinary contest not far from the city, which ended in the total defeat of his troops by the parliamentary forces. In that day's struggle, and in the Siege that followed it, many a Chester hero bit the dust; and the roll-call that evening proclaimed many an infant fatherless, many a wife a widow! But why should we anticipate? We shall soon be close to the very walls of this Tower, and may then soliloquise to our heart's content on those terrible times.

For the present, then, we will move on along Frodsham Street, anciently called Cowlane, pausing midway to reflect that in the Quakers' Meeting-house, at the corner of Union Walk, Friend William Penn, the founder of Pennsylvania, held forth to his admirers, King James II. being on one occasion an attentive hearer. Continuing on our course a short distance, we emerge from Cowlane into a wide but irregular street, named indifferently FOREST or FOREGATE STREET, the latter, from its standing immediately before the gate,—the EASTGATE, close by, being always esteemed *the porta principalis* of the city. Foregate Street forms a part of the old Watling Street of the Romans; so that it existed as a road almost as early as the crucifixion of Our Lord! Fifty years ago this was as curious a street as any within the city; but the ancient piazzas which once ran continuously along it, are now becoming mere specks in the landscape, and "like angels' visits, few and far between." Not far from where we are standing, near the corner of St. John's Street, are two superior travellers' inns, the HOPPOLE, and the BLOSSOMS, the latter a house of the highest standing and respectability, admirably adapted for the accommodation of visitors, and for all those who would enjoy the comfort of a home combined with the advantages of a first-class HOTEL. At the rear of the Blossoms, in St. John Street, is the POST OFFICE, a neat stuccoed building, erected in 1842, at the sole expense of William Palin, Esq., the present post-master. Prior to this, the business of the Post-Office was conducted in a dark and dreary building, situate up a court, still known as the Old Post-Office Yard. It was to Rowland Hill, and his wonder-working penny stamp, that the citizens owed this satisfactory change from darkness unto light.

Foregate Street, and Blossoms' Hotel.

Yonder white stone building at the head of St. John Street is the well-known banking establishment of Messrs. Williams & Co., usually denominated the Old Bank. And, here, crossing the street at an altitude of some thirty feet, is the EASTGATE, a noble arch, with a postern on either side, erected in 1769, on the site of a Gateway, dating back to the days of the Third Edward, by Robert, first Marquis of Westminster, whose arms, with those of the city, ornament the keystone of the centre arch.

Handsome and commodious as is the present EASTGATE,—on every score but that of convenience, it is immeasurably inferior to its predecessor. Could we but look upon the structure as it existed only a hundred years ago, with its beautiful Gothic archway, flanked by two massive octagonal towers, four stories in height, supporting the Gate itself and the rooms above,—could we but resuscitate the time-worn embattlements of that "ancient of days," we should wonder at and pity the spurious taste that decreed its fall. "Oh, but," we may be told, "the present Gate was a public improvement." A plague upon such improvements, say we! We should vastly have preferred, and so would every lover of the antique, whether citizen or stranger, to have retained the old Gate in its integrity, altered, had need been, to meet the growing wants of the times, rather than have thus consigned it to the ruthless hands of the destroyer. Oh! ye spirits of the valiant dead,—you who lost your lives defending this Gate against the cannons of Cromwell, why did ye not rise up from your graves, and arrest the mad course of that "age of improvement!" When this Gate was being demolished, the massive arches of the original Roman structure were laid bare to the view, and a portion of one of them is yet to be seen on the north-west side of the present Gateway.

At this point we will turn away from the street, and, ascending the steps on the north-east side, will amuse ourselves in the next chapter with a quiet WALK ROUND THE WALLS OF CHESTER.

CHAPTER III.

The Walls of Chester, their builders and their history.—The Cathedral.—The Phœnix Tower, and the Walls during the Siege.—Beeston Castle.—The North Gate.—Training College.—Morgan's Mount and Pemberton's Parlour.—The Water Tower.—Infirmary and Gaol.—Linen Hall.—The Watergate.

A WALK round the Walls of Chester! Now, then, for a choice *tête-à-tête* with the past! Away with the commonplace nineteenth century! Away with the mammon-loving world of to-day! The path we are now treading, high above the busy haunts of men, has a traditional halo and interest peculiarly its own.

With the rapidity of thought, our imagination wanders some eighteen hundred years backwards on the stream of time, to the days when Marius, King of the Britons, to defend his royal city from the incursions of his enemies, built up a fortified wall around Chester. The Britons, however, were no masons; and their rude defences availed them little when opposed to the resistless career of Rome. Surrendered to its new masters, the Romans, Chester speedily gave unmistakeable evidence of the change. The mud-walls, or earthworks of the conquered, vanished before the imperial masonry of the conquerors; and the Walls of Chester, built as only Roman hands could build them, rose majestically in their place, clasping the city in an embrace of stone, defiant alike of time and of the foe.

Chester Walls, which afford a continuous promenade, nearly two miles in circumference, are the only perfect specimen of that order of ancient fortification now remaining in Britain. The Walls of Shrewsbury, York, and other places that occur to us, though interesting enough in their way, yet "hide their diminished heads" beside the proud old ramparts of Chester. Where is the pen or the pencil that can depict the scenes of glory and renown, so inseparably bound up with the history of these Walls? For three or four centuries the Roman soldier kept watch and ward over them, and over the city; but no sooner had their legions withdrawn from Britain, than the whole island was shaken to its centre by the ruthless invasion of the Picts and Goths. Deserted by their old protectors, the Britons invoked the aid of the Saxons, under Hengist and Horsa; who, landing at the head of a powerful army, in concert with the Britons, soon drove the invaders from their quarters within the Walls of Chester.

The Saxons in turn, perceiving the weakness of the unfortunate Britons, determined on possessing themselves of the country; and, during the conflict that ensued, Chester was frequently taken and retaken by the respective belligerents, and many a fierce and bloody battle raged beneath its Walls. In 607, for instance, Ethelred, King of Northumberland, laid siege to the city; and, after a sanguinary struggle outside the Walls, during which he put one thousand two hundred British monks to the sword, wrested the city from its native defenders. Again, however, the Britons returned to the rescue; and, driving out the usurpers, retained possession of Chester for more than two hundred years.

The Danes were the next invaders of old Chester; but, about the year 908, Ethelred, Earl of Mercia, and Ethelfleda, his countess, restored the shattered Walls and Gates of the city; in which state they remained,

> Bristling with spears, and bright with burnish'd shields,

through many a long and eventful epoch of England's history, Chester's faithful safeguard against every foe. In what good stead they availed the city during the trying period of the great CIVIL WAR, a former chapter has sufficiently declared; and, though we cannot but rejoice that those days of anarchy and confusion have passed away, yet are we sure, should the direful necessity again arise, the hearts of the men of Chester will still beat as loyally, and their stalwart arms emulate as nobly, the glorious deeds of their forefathers of yore! And now for our proposed Walk round these celebrated Walls.

The steps we have just ascended give us but poor "first impressions" of the Walls, the view being blocked up on either side by most unpicturesque buildings. But when we have proceeded northward a few steps, a prospect of venerable magnificence suddenly reveals itself. To our left, and so close that we can hear the organ pealing forth its joyous hallelujahs, we have a splendid view of the CATHEDRAL of St. Werburgh, seen here, perhaps, to greater advantage than from any other accessible point. The first glance will show us that it is a cruciform structure, as most of our cathedrals are, the massive and weather-beaten tower standing just in the centre compartment of the cross. The left wing, though an integral portion of the building, is, nevertheless, a separate parish church, dedicated to ST. OSWALD. The choir itself occupies the entire range of the edifice between us and the tower, the *Chapel of Our Ladye* being in the immediate foreground. At our feet lie numberless memorials of the dead, which—

> With uncouth rhymes and shapeless sculpture deck'd,
> Implore the passing tribute of a sigh.

This ground has served for a place of sepulture almost since the Conquest, and has only recently been closed by act of parliament.

Deferring our special notice of the Cathedral, until "a more convenient season," we shortly find ourselves at the end of Abbey Street, and immediately over the KALEYARDS GATE. This postern leads to the cabbage and kale gardens, which formerly belonged to the Abbot and Convent of St. Werburgh. The opening was permitted to be made for their convenience in the reign of Edward I. to prevent the necessity of bringing their vegetables by a circuitous route through the East Gate. The "good things" in vogue among these reverend fathers were not, it is evident, wholly spiritual. A defunct ropery, timberyard, and infant school now flourish on the spot where monkish cabbages and conventual kale in old time grew.

A few paces farther on was a quadrangular abutment, on which formerly stood a tower called *The Sadlers' Tower*, from its having been the meeting-room of the Company of Sadlers. This tower was taken down in 1780; and the abutment, which marked the place where it stood, was demolished in 1828.

We are now at an interesting portion of the Walls. Do you see that mouldering old turret some fifty yards a-head of us? Three hundred years ago it was familiarly known as Newton's Tower; but the men of the present day call it the PHŒNIX TOWER, from the figure of the phœnix, which is the crest of one of the city companies, ornamenting the front of the structure. Look up, as we approach it, and read, over its elevated portal, the startling announcement, that

> KING CHARLES
> STOOD ON THIS TOWER
> SEPTEMBER 24th, 1645, AND SAW
> HIS ARMY DEFEATED
> ON ROWTON MOOR.

Let us mount the rugged steps, and having reached the summit, gaze awhile on the beautiful scene before us.

Phœnix Tower, from the Canal.

To our left is the suburb of Newtown, a creation of the present century,—the modest little spire of Christ Church pointing to the thoughtful wayfarer another and a better world. Yonder, just visible above the intervening buildings, the noble façade of the Railway Station arrests the eye. Farther to the right, the Lead Works' Shot Tower again presents itself; while beneath us, at a depth of about forty feet, the sleepy Canal flows languidly along, scarce a ripple distracting its glassy surface. The bridge that crosses it is Cowlane Bridge, whence we obtained the first glimpse of the Cathedral, *en route* from the station. Just over the canal is the new CATTLE MARKET, the Cestrian Smithfield,—translated hither from Northgate Street in 1849. That heavy-looking building just over the Bridge is the Independent Chapel in Queen Street; while full south, the lofty steeple and church of St. John "lend enchantment to the view." Beyond all these, some ten or a dozen miles away, the rocky heights of Beeston salute the eye, capped with the ruins of a Castle, built by Earl Randle Blundeville,—a fortress which was several times taken and retaken by the Royalists and Roundheads in the great Civil War. To the right again, the stately form of the fine old Cathedral, like a nursing mother, watches peacefully o'er the city. THE WALLS beneath us are full of interest to the archæologist, for through almost their entire length between this Tower and the Eastgate, the old Roman masonry may yet be distinguished, forming the lower courses nearest the foundations.

As we once more look up, and read yon quaint yet melancholy inscription, our minds will of necessity revert back to that sad September day, when Charles the First stood on this very spot and saw his gallant cavaliers borne down by the grim soldiers of Oliver Cromwell's army. For three years he had maintained a doubtful contest with his Parliament; and though for a time the successes of his troops in the western counties had given a fitful gleam of prosperity to his sinking fortunes, the tide had now turned, and one disaster followed another in quick succession. On the fields of Naseby and Marston Moor he had been signally defeated. Bristol had fallen; Prince Rupert had been disgraced and sent beyond the seas; and the prospect daily grew darker. Chester remained firm; and hither Charles had come to encourage his loyal subjects, and give to the battle which seemed inevitable, the cheering influence of his kingly presence. The city had been besieged for some months, and the houses in the suburbs were mostly destroyed.

On the 23rd of September the King entered Chester; and the next day his troops gave battle to the Parliamentary forces. Charles, with Sir Francis Gamull the Mayor, here watched the progress of the contest; and when at last all hope was gone, and his soldiers fled before the fiery Puritans, he turned from the melancholy spectacle, descended the steps of this Tower, and the next day with great difficulty made his escape from the city. This defeat was but the precursor of worse misfortunes. Within three years from that day, a crowd was gathered in front of the Palace at Whitehall. A man in a mask severed at one blow, the King's head from his body, and another, holding up the ghastly countenance to the view of the weeping spectators, cried aloud, "This is the head of a traitor!" England was not many years discovering who were the real traitors.

Charles had left Chester in worthy hands. "If you do not receive relief in eight days," said he to Lord Byron, who was in command, "surrender the garrison." The appointed time passed away, but no relief came. Day after day for four months, the citizens of Chester, with a courage and determination that claim our admiration, refused the oft-repeated summons to surrender. But there was an enemy within the walls, far more formidable than the troops without. Famine proved more powerful than the sword. When the provisions were exhausted, as a last resource the horses were slaughtered and given out in small rations. Dogs and cats were eaten as dainties; and many of the inhabitants perished from the dreadful hardships which were brought to their homes. The men were not alone in this gallant defence. "The women," says an old chronicler, "like so many valiant Amazons, do out-face death and dare danger, though it lurk in every basket; seven are shot and three slain—yet they scorn to leave their matchless undertaking, and thus they continue for ten days' space; possessing the beholders that they are immortal." At last, reduced to the utmost extremity, and all hope of relief being gone, the city surrendered on condition that the public and private buildings should be unharmed by the Parliamentary troops. The churches still bear melancholy witness to the manner in which this solemn compact was regarded; and the organ and choir of the Cathedral were broken and defaced, with a Vandalism whose traces yet tell of the horrors of civil war.

So much then for the Phœnix Tower, and its historical associations. We must now move on to the westward, taking note on our way of UPTON CHURCH and spire, lying just upon the northern confines of the city.

Below us stretches away the CANAL, which, here usurping the place of the ancient *fosse*, skirts the entire city, within the Walls, from east to west. Bidding a friendly adieu to the Dean's Field, that beautiful mead on our left, we approach by a slight incline the NORTH GATE of the city. Look now over the right-hand parapet upon the yawning gulf below, and reflect that, while yon arch was built by an architect of our own time, that course of stones beneath us—the dark ones between the ivy and the abutment—was laid by a Roman mason, when Rome herself was mistress of the world.

Ascending two or three steps, we find ourselves on the top of the NORTH GATE, which here, with its neat elliptical arch, divides Upper from Lower North Gate Street. That new-looking red-brick building beneath us is the BLUE-COAT HOSPITAL, a charity school, under the same roof with the ancient Hospital of St. John,—of both which institutions more anon.

Pass we on now still to the westward, until we come to a curious watch-tower, called MORGAN'S MOUNT, having a lower chamber on the level of the Walls, and an open platform above, accessible by a few winding steps. During the Siege of Chester, a battery was planted on the summit of this tower, and from its commanding position, surrounded by earthworks, successfully kept the besiegers at bay. Let us mount to the top, and survey the diversified prospect before us. See yonder Elizabethan building at the northwest extremity of the city, beautifully placed on a hill, and separated from us by those fine, dark, evergreen trees, through which you can see the bright sunshine, as it were, smiling approvingly upon it. It is the Diocesan TRAINING COLLEGE, a normal establishment, for preparing masters and teachers for the parochial schools of the diocese. Stretching away to our left is the Hundred of Wirrall, the foreground dotted here and there with a handsome mansion or substantial farm-house, among which those of Crabwall, Mollington, and Blacon, are most conspicuous. That house, so sweetly situate on the eminence to the left, embowered in trees, is Blacon Point, commanding extensive views of the city and North Wales. Still beneath us flows the Canal, which, however, empties itself, close at hand, by a series of descending locks, into the River Dee. That pile of buildings on the opposite bank of the Canal, is the central official establishment of the Shropshire Union Railway Company. The River Dee, the mountains of

North Wales, and the ancient Walls, serve nobly to complete this glowing panorama of nature, and of art.

Once more, forward!—but only for a few steps; for here we are arrived at another Tower, originally twice its present height, and at one time denominated the *Goblin's Tower* (doubtless for some *ghostly* reason), but of late better known as PEMBERTON'S PARLOUR. Though now semicircular, this was, in all probability, a round or octagonal tower when first erected, having a passage through for pedestrians. Be that as it may, in 1702, being in a ruinous state, a great part of it was taken down, and the remainder repaired. The side towards the Walls was refaced and ornamented with some fine heraldic sculpture; and an inscription, now almost obliterated, proclaimed that in a certain "year of the glorious reign of Queen Anne, divers wide breaches in these Walls were re-built, and other decays therein were repaired; 2000 yards of the pavement were new flagged or paved, and the whole repaired, regulated, and adorned, at the expense of £1000 and upwards. Thomas Hand, Esq., Mayor, 1701. The Right Honourable William, Earl of Derby, Mayor, 1702, who died in his Mayoralty."

Pemberton's Parlour and City Walls.

Passing on from ivy-capt *Pemberton's Parlour*, we see on our left hand, through that refreshing grove of trees, a large and verdant mead, still retaining its ancient name of the *Barrow Field*, or *Lady Barrow's Hay*. This is the place where the soldiers of old Rome went through their daily military exercises, and where, 500 years afterwards, great numbers of the citizens who died of the plague were hurriedly interred. We are now upon a flat iron Bridge, and whew! with a rush like that of a tiger from his den, the giant of the nineteenth century—a steam-engine and train—emerge from the dark tunnel which passes under the city, and dash away beneath us, full forty miles an hour, *en route* to Ireland, by way of Holyhead. The Roman Walls, that resisted so successfully the Roundhead batteries, have in our own times succumbed to the engines of peace, and the railway trains, with their living freight, now career it merrily through two neighbouring apertures in these ancient fortifications.

A little farther ahead are some modern steps, leading down to the new BATHS and WASHHOUSES, in which is a capacious swimming-bath, where plebeians may indulge in a plunge for a penny, and where hot and cold shower and vapour baths are at the service of the public on equally reasonable terms. Previous to the erection of these Baths, the only means of egress from the city at this point was by an ancient postern underneath us, now blocked up.

Wheeling sharp round to the left, for the Walls here take a direction southward, we cross a second Railway Bridge, and then turn to regale ourselves with an immediate foreground of startling interest. We are looking upon a Tower erected in 1322, by one Helpstone, a mason, who contracted to build it for 100*l.*, a high price in those days, when workmen for their day's wage, "received but every man his penny." It consists of a higher and lower tower, the former being distinguished by the break jaw name of *Bonewaldesthorne's Tower*, and connected by a steep flight of steps and an embattled terrace with the lower or WATER TOWER. This tower was erected while the tidal waters of the Dee flowed up to Chester Walls; and within the memory of man the rings and bolts were to be seen about the old turret, to which, centuries ago, the ships that came up to the city were safely moored. The case is altered now, and, thanks to the duplicity of a public company, "Deva's wizard stream" ebbs and flows almost in vain for "rare old Chester." "Stone walls tell no tales," says the proverb; but yon crumbling old ruin, so stern, so ragged, so venerable to look upon, tells us in plain though silent language its own unvarnished tale. Look at its broken and serrated surface, its disfigured battlements? Think you old Time alone has wrought all this? Turn to the annals of the city, and there read that the Roundhead battery on Bruera's Hall hill yonder played its artillery fiercely against this tower during the great Civil War; and though its fair form was shattered, its buttresses shaken by the terrible cannonade, yet the proud old structure remained intact, and the hearts of its defenders unfaltering, through the whole of that fierce and lamentable struggle. The scenes then enacted have passed away, as we hope for ever, and this venerable stronghold has become subservient to another and more peaceful purpose, as a local and general antiquarian MUSEUM. Of course we must go in and examine it for ourselves, and think, as we do so, with becoming honour of the gallant spirits who once kept watch and ward over its safety. It will cost us just sixpence each to pass in; but never mind that, were the charge a crown, it would not have been money injudiciously thrown away.

The Water Tower, Railway, and City Walls.

The room we have passed into is the ancient keep, formerly known as BONEWALDESTHORNE'S TOWER; and after ruminating a moment on the rusty swords and rapiers that hang around, we will mount the winding staircase into the room above. Here, on a whitened table, the light of day being first excluded, we are introduced to the wondrous revelations of the CAMERA OBSCURA. On this little table we have pourtrayed, with minute but pleasing accuracy, every place and occurrence within gunshot of the Tower,—boats on the Canal, pedestrians on the Walls, ships on the Dee, green fields and trees, the flying train, and every passing incident, ridiculous or sublime. From this Tower we proceed by a steep descent of zig-zag steps, between rugged battlements of venerable sandstone, thickly coated with "that rare old plant, the ivy green," to the centre of attraction, the WATER TOWER itself. How beautiful, how indescribably beautiful, are those thick masses of dark, glossy, green ivy, "creeping where no life is seen" round the blackened old ramparts we have just passed by!

The iron gate or portcullis opens at our approach, and we enter a spacious room, once bristling with hosts of armed men, but now filled with curiosities and natural productions from every quarter of the globe. A corkscrew staircase brings us to a similar room on the second story; while higher still, upon the leads of the Tower, where the stalwart warrior once paced his silent round, the observant visitor may feast his eyes on a varied scene of wood and dale, mountain and river, garden and field, of surpassing interest. To give anything like a detail of the curiosities and antiquities stored up in this Tower would fill an ordinary volume; let it suffice, then, to point out a few of the more prominent and striking. Here is a large and beautiful collection of shells, scientifically arranged, the gift of Captain T. L. Massie, R.N., and there a case of Australian birds, presented to the Museum by another worthy citizen. In yonder glass-case we have, at one view, specimens of almost every known variety of British birds, from the majestic bittern to the diminutive jenny wren. Here is the "old arm-chair" of Bishop Goodman, one of the worthiest prelates of our renowned Queen Bess. Here again are trophies of battle and victory from Inkermann and Alma; and there are glass cases of Greek, Roman, and British coins, from the penny bearing the "image and superscription of Cæsar," to the chaste medallions of our own beloved Queen. There, too, is the skull of a soldier killed during the Civil War, in the neighbourhood of Beeston Castle, the deadly impress of two flattened bullets being still visible on the skull. Those blackened fragments you are now surveying are the hand and foot of an Egyptian mummy, the owner of which may possibly have been a contemporary of Pharaoh. Doubtless this mummy, when in life, was a confirmed old maid; for see, here is her favourite *cat*, embalmed like herself, and found by her side when she was exhumed. The cat was a sacred animal with the ancient Egyptians. We might linger here profitably a whole day, but having other fish to fry, we must bid farewell to the Water Tower and its obliging attendants, and remounting the lofty steps, find ourselves once more on the venerable Walls.

Resuming now our walk, we approach a large and handsome brick building, on the city side of the Walls. This is the Chester INFIRMARY, and a most useful and valuable institution it is, having been founded in 1755 by Dr. Stratford, of Chester, and supported entirely by the contributions of the charitable in Cheshire and North Wales. The present structure was erected in 1761, and has accommodation under its roof for one hundred patients, besides spacious hot, cold, and vapour baths, and all the usual adjuncts of a first class hospital. The upper story on the north side of the building is set apart for a fever ward; and in this, as in every other beneficial arrangement, the Chester Infirmary is second to none in the kingdom. The honorary medical staff consists of three physicians and three surgeons; and from these, and the worthy house surgeon and matron, the patients receive the utmost assistance that human kindness and skill can bestow. The halt and maimed, the sick and dying of the poorer classes are here watched with anxious care, and experience comforts to which at home or elsewhere they would necessarily be strangers.

The Infirmary was founded for the eradication of one species of evils; but here is a building for the suppression of evils of another description. The CITY GAOL, for such is the gloomy-looking structure before us, is an erection of the present century, having supplanted the old and ruinous prison which formerly stood upon the site of the present North Gate. Over the handsome Doric entrance is an iron railing, within which the last sentence of the law is occasionally executed on condemned criminals. Surely the day is not far distant when "death by the hangman" will be a punishment unknown to the criminal code of England! What adds to the evil, so far as Chester is concerned, is that the authorities of the City are compelled, by some antediluvian charter, to see execution done on every condemned criminal within the County, though for what reason this especial *honour* was first conferred on the citizens, is an enigma susceptible of no clear solution.

A short distance hence is Stanley Place, a double row of genteel residences; at the head of which, within that ponderous gateway, is the old LINEN HALL, once the great mart for Irish linens, but of late, owing to the decay of that branch of trade, consecrated to the sale of the famed Cheshire cheese. What! have you never yet tasted a bit of "prime old Cheshire?" Let us recommend you then to do so, on your return to the Inn; and if your fancy does not gloat over it for a month or two to come, our belief in your *good taste* will be considerably modified.

"Onward!" is again the word, and ascending a short incline, we find ourselves on the top of another of the four great Gates of the city. We are now exactly opposite to where we set out, and have, therefore, at least half completed our circuit of the city. The West, or as it is more usually termed, the WATER GATE (from the Dee having originally flowed up to its portals), is like the East and North Gates, a modern structure, having replaced the old and unsightly archway in 1789, as appears by an inscription on the west side. The custody of Chester Gates was at one time a privilege much courted by the high and mighty in the land. Thus the sergeantship of the East Gate has belonged since the time of Edward I. to the ancestors of the present Lord Crewe, of Crewe; the North Gate during that period has been in charge of the citizens; the Water Gate, on which we are now standing, in custody of the Stanleys, Earls of Derby; while the Bridge Gate, to which we shall presently come, belonged to the Earls of Shrewsbury, inheriting from their ancestors, the Troutbecks and Rabys, sergeants thereof in the fourteenth century. Below us lies a plain of sweetest verdure and most inviting beauty; and by way of diversifying our subject, we will now step down from the Gate and Walls, and find ourselves, in another chapter, treading the green sward of the old Roodeye.

CHAPTER IV.

The Walls, continued.—The Roodeye.—Chester Races.—The Castle of the Olden Time, and the Castle of To-day.—The Grosvenor Bridge.—Cæsar's Tower.—Handbridge and Edgar's Cave.—Bridgegate.—Dee Mills and Bridge.—Causeway.—Queen's Park and Wishing Steps.—The Newgate and its Traditions.—The East Gate.

WELL, here we are, on a beautiful meadow, eighty-four acres in extent, clad in Nature's own mantle of brightest green, and bearing the euphonious name of the ROODEYE. This splendid pasture, now so cheerful to look upon, has not always worn the same gay aspect. In ages past and gone—when the Saxon and the Norman held sway over the land—when colossal Liverpool was but a simple fishing-hamlet—the infant commerce of England was borne along the surging billows of the Dee, up to the very Walls of Chester. In those days the spacious lawn before us was covered with water at every tide, save only a bank or eye of land near the centre, which being surmounted by a plain substantial stone cross, acquired the name of the ROODEYE, or the *Island of the Cross*. Are you fond of legends?—Here then is one that may gratify your taste.

Once upon a time (you must not ask *when*) the Christians of Hawarden, a few miles down the river, were in a sad strait for lack of rain. Now it so happened that in the church of that place there stood an image of the Virgin Mary, called Holy Rood. To her shrine then repaired the faithful and fearful of all classes to pray for rain. Among the rest, Lady Trawst, the wife of the governor of Hawarden, prayed so heartily and so long, that the image, grown desperate we suppose, fell down upon the lady and killed her. Mad with rage at this "answer to their prayers," a jury of the inhabitants was summoned, and the Holy Rood summarily convicted of wilful murder and other heinous sins. Fearful, however, of the consequences if they executed the offender, the jury determined to lay her upon the beach at low water; whence the next tide carried her away to the spot where she was found, under the Walls of Chester. The citizens held a *post-mortem* examination, and seeing that she was *Holy Rood*, decided on burying her where she was found, and erected over her a simple stone Cross, which, tradition says, once bore an inscription to the following effect:

> The Jews their God did crucify,
>   The Hardeners theirs did drown:
> Because their wants she'd not supply,—
>   And she lies under this cold stone.

Another version affirms she was carried to ST. JOHN'S CHURCH, and there set up in great pomp, and that this Cross was erected on the spot where she was found.

So much for the legend: yonder is the remnant of the Cross under which her holiness was laid; and as

> Little she'll reck, if they'll let her sleep on,
> We will leave her alone in her glory.

The spot now marks the boundary of St. Mary's parish. The athletic sports and Olympian games of the Romans, the military displays of the Edwards and Henries, the pageants and plays of the sixteenth and seventeenth centuries, were each in their day "set forth" on the Roodeye before hundreds of wondering and admiring citizens. And it is pretty much the same "even in this our day;" for martial reviews and rejoicings, cricket and other athletic games are all celebrated and fostered on its rich green sward.

Why, it was only the other day, on the 2nd of April, 1856, that the rank and beauty of the county (and that beauty does reign dominant in Cheshire all the world knows) assembled on the ROODEYE to witness a grand and exciting ceremonial. For two years war had been convulsing Europe; Turkey the weak had been marked out for a prey by Russia the strong; the Eagle of the North would have trampled on the Crescent, and have blotted out its name from the catalogue of nations. But the British lion looked on from afar,—the champion of the weak girded on its ancient strength,—and with the aid of France, once its enemy, but now a gallant ally, went forth to the rescue. The result is patent to the world. In two short years the pride of the despot has been humbled, and the freedom of his almost victim assured, while Peace once again spreads its mantle over the earth. The militia of England formed the nursery at home for the army abroad; and the militia of Cheshire in particular responded nobly to the repeated demands of their country. No wonder, then, that the Roodeye was so crowded and gay on the occasion in question,—that so many desired to witness the presentation of new banners to the gallant 1st Regiment of Royal Cheshire Militia. The Marchioness of Westminster, as the representative of the Lord Lieutenant, presented the colours, which were first duly consecrated by the amiable Bishop of the diocese. *We* were present at the ceremony; and, as the ensigns of the regiment received their handsome banners, and unfurled them to the breeze, we felt a glow of pride upon our cheek that the ancient chivalry of Cheshire still animated her loyal sons. England has once more had to learn, and will surely not this time forget the lesson, that "the only way to be certain of peace, is to be at all times amply prepared for war."

Grand Stand, and Water Gate.

But the Roodeye is perhaps chiefly famous for the splendid horse Races which are twice a-year held here; and while the course itself is a perfect amphitheatre, and the spectator's view of the contests magnificent and unbroken, it is not too much to say, that the fame of CHESTER RACES is a household word with every true lover of old English sports. Our illustration presents to us a view of the handsome GRAND STAND, with the Walls and Water Gate on the left; but for a more general view of the entire race-course, we may profitably refer to the frontispiece at the commencement of our GUIDE. The viaduct on the extreme left is, with the girder-bridge over the Dee, the iron road of communication between England and Ireland; while beyond it, again, lies the "Port of Chester;" as also the ROODEYE GAS WORKS, WORKHOUSE, and last, not least, the iron shipbuilding yard, conducted by Mr. Cram, of this city.

We will now return to the WALLS, noticing as we pass through the Water Gate, to the right, the remains of the wall of the *Black Friars' Monastery*. Proceeding southward a short distance, we arrive at a field, on the left hand, in which formerly stood the Benedictine *Nunnery of St. Mary*. Within living memory, portions of this conventual establishment were visible from the Walls, but all traces thereof are now unfortunately obliterated. We have here a pretty close view of the CASTLE, SAVINGS BANK, and ST. BRIDGET'S CHURCH; but as we have now arrived at the New, or Grosvenor Road, we will approach still nearer, and while surveying and admiring the Castle of the present, ruminate a little on the Castle of past days.

When Chester Castle was first erected, whether during the British, Roman or Saxon occupation, is a problem likely never to be determined. There can be no question, however, that it existed some time previous to the Norman

Conquest; for it was the chosen court and camp of Hugh Lupus the Norman, nephew of the Conqueror, and is stated by Camden to have been merely *repaired* by that powerful baron. On the death of the last Norman Earl, the Castle passed into the hands of the king (Henry III.).

"Henry of Lancaster, (afterwards Henry IV.) having taken up arms against Richard II., in 1399, mustered his army upon the banks of the Dee, under the Walls of Chester, and Sir Piers Legh of Lyme, an adherent of Richard, was beheaded, and his head set upon the top of the highest tower in the Castle. A few days afterwards, the unfortunate Richard and the Earl of Salisbury were brought prisoners to Chester, mounted (says Hall) 'upon two little nagges, not worth forty francs,' when the King was delivered 'to the Duke of Gloucester's sonne and the Earle of Arundell's sonne, that loved him but a little, for he had put their fathers to death, who led him strait to the Castell.'

"In 1403, Henry Percy, the renowned Hotspur, visited Chester, on his way to the fatal field of Shrewsbury, and caused proclamation to be made, that King Richard was yet alive, and a prisoner in Chester Castle, where he might be seen.

"Eleanor, Duchess of Gloucester, wife of the *Good Duke Humphrey*, was confined for several months in Chester Castle, in 1447, previous to her removal to the Isle of Man, under a sentence of perpetual imprisonment on a charge of 'practising the King's death.'

"Here, in 1651, the Puritans *'sought the Lord'* by trying and condemning to death the gallant and patriotic Earl of Derby, Sir Timothy Featherstonehaugh, and Captain Benbow. According to Whitlocke, the Earl 'attempted to escape, and was let down by a rope from the leads of his chamber; but some hearing a noise, made after him, and he was re-taken upon Dee bank.' He was afterwards beheaded at Bolton, while Featherstonehaugh was shot in the market-place of Chester."

And now for the Castle of the present day. The old structure was removed towards the close of the eighteenth century, and the new one erected from the plans of the late Thomas Harrison, Esq., the architect of the Grosvenor Bridge.

The GRAND ENTRANCE occupies the centre of a semicircular fosse, and is of the Grecian Doric order. The whole of the majestic fluted columns of this Gateway and of the Shire Hall, are constructed each, from capital to base, of a single stone. As we pass into the CASTLE YARD, we have at one view a fine prospect of this noble square.

"The two wings of the Castle, and the whole of the buildings to the right, are appropriated to the military; the centre to the Assize Court and County

Gaol. The right wing is the officer's barracks. There are at present in this Castle, a regiment of militia, and a battalion of artillery. The pensioners' offices are at the back of the left wing, at one side of which is the Nisi Prius Court, Grand Jury Room, &c.

"The first floor of the new barracks on the higher wards is appropriated to the *Armoury*, which contains 30,000 stand of arms, and is decorated with various devices, formed solely of weapons of warfare.

"Near these buildings is an old Square Tower, called *Julius Cæsar's*, otherwise *Julius Agricola's Tower*, in which was situated the *Chantry of St. Mary infra Castrum*. It was in this Chapel that James II. received Mass during his stay in Chester. This Tower was built soon after the Norman Conquest. There was an ancient fresco painting on the interior walls, the subject of which was Moses receiving the Table of Commandments from the Mount, whilst the Devil in a nondescript form is trying to seize them; in the background are his old friends *the Pope*, and a group of ecclesiastical personages. This Tower was newly cased with red stone in 1818. The Powder Magazine is at present kept in it." Close by stood, prior to its demolition, the ancient Shire Hall and Exchequer Court: the latter was the parliament house of the palatinate earls, and had neat carved seats for the earl and his eight barons, spiritual and temporal.

Castle, Shire Hall, and Cæsar's Tower.

"As before stated, the centre buildings contain the Assize Court and City Gaol. In front of the Hall of Justice is a portico, supported by twelve pillars in double rows. The entrances are at the sides of the portico. The interior of the Court is of a semicircular form, forty-four feet high, eighty feet diameter, and forty-four feet wide. Round the semicircle is a colonnade of twelve Ionic pillars, supporting a semi-dome, divided into four square compartments, richly embellished. The *tout ensemble* is grand

and imposing, and admirably adapted to give a majestic appearance to a judicial court.

"Behind this building is the Constable's residence, a terrace in front of which commands a view of the Chapel, and Felons' Yards below, five in number. The Debtors' Yards form quadrangles on the right and left of the Constable's house, on a level with the Castle Yard."

The Churches of St. Mary, and St. Bridget, are both within a stone's throw; but we must leave them for the present, and continue our interesting "Walk round the Walls." In a few minutes we arrive at the angle of the Walls, where the massive ramparts of the Castle frown majestically above us, while below, the classic waters of the Dee flow languidly on, regardless of yon noble and magnificent stone Bridge, which, with its unequalled single arch of 200 feet span, crosses the river a short distance away from us. This is the GROSVENOR BRIDGE, finished in 1832, at a cost of 30,000*l.* and formally opened in October of that year, by Her present Most Gracious Majesty, then Princess Victoria. It has the reputation of being the *largest stone arch in the world.* Immediately to the left of the Bridge is the Cemetery, of which more hereafter.

Again we pass onwards, having on our left the higher wards of the Castle, Julius Cæsar's Tower, and the lofty boundary wall of the new County Gaol. Cæsar's Tower (so called) has of late years been converted into a powder magazine, and may, some day or other, make itself both heard and felt by the citizens, unless they procure the removal of the magazine to some more distant and fitting locality.

Still onwards, by the side of the Dee, and we approach the Old Dee Bridge and Mills, having on the opposite shore the suburb of HANDBRIDGE, called by the Welsh *Treboeth*, or *burnt town*, from its having been so often razed to the ground during their predatory incursions. Yonder is EDGAR'S FIELD, so called from the palace of that Saxon monarch having been traditionally situate there. In this field is a projecting rock, partially excavated, still bearing the name of EDGAR'S CAVE; and the tradition is that, in 971, that monarch was rowed from thence to St. John's Church by six petty kings or princes, in token of their subjection to his rule. At the entrance of the cave is a rude sculpture, supposed to represent Minerva, accompanied by her usual symbol, the owl.

Where we are now standing was, fifty years ago, an ancient postern, called the SHIPGATE, or *Sheepgate*, from which went a ford across the river into Handbridge. The gate itself, of Roman construction, on being taken down, was carefully preserved, and now ornaments the garden of the present town clerk, J. Finchett-Maddock, Esq., in Abbey Square.

A few steps further will bring us to the South or BRIDGE GATE, the last of the four principal Gates of the city. It is a bold and imposing structure, erected, in 1782, at the expense of the corporation, in place of the old and ponderous gateway which previously occupied its site. The old Gate is quoted in deeds as far back as the twelfth century, and appears to have been granted by the Norman Earl Randle and his Countess to one Poyns, their servant, for some meritorious but unrecorded service. From his successors it passed, through Philip le Clerc, to the families of Raby, Norris, and Troutbeck, until the honour of "custodian of the Bridge Gate" became vested at length in the Earls of Shrewsbury, who, in the seventeenth century, sold their rights to the Corporation.

Crossing over the Bridge Gate, we have now a better view of the DEE MILLS, a massive pile of buildings, resting on the south-west end of the Old Bridge. The Dee Mills existed on this very spot shortly after the Norman Conquest, and were for centuries a source of immense revenue to their owners, the Earls. Edward the Black Prince, as Earl of Chester, granted them for life to Sir Howel-y-Fwyal, constable of Criccaeth Castle, for his gallant conduct at the Battle of Poictiers; since which time they have passed through successive owners to the Wrench family, who are the present possessors. The Mills have been thrice destroyed by fire.

The DEE BRIDGE is of great antiquity, having been erected in 1280 by the citizens, under a peremptory order to that effect from King Edward I. Previous to that date there had been a *wooden bridge* here, originating with that amazonian "edifier" of Chester, the Mercian Princess Ethelfleda; but that passage was continually subject to interruptions, both from the violence of the tides, and the restless zeal of the Welshmen,—hence the erection of the present Bridge. It consists at present of seven arches of irregular size, but is said to have originally boasted of two or three more, now built up. It was widened in 1826, by the addition of a projecting footpath, seven feet wide, which has somewhat destroyed its antiquated appearance from this point of view.

The CAUSEWAY, or weir, on this side the Bridge, is recorded to have been first built by Hugh Lupus, the Conqueror's nephew, probably about the time of the foundation of the Dee Mills. It stemmed the tide of the Dee, and of all opposition, until the period of the Commonwealth, when we find an order of parliament commanding the destruction of both Causeway and Mills; but the puritanical order appears to have been derisively set at nought; at all events, it was never carried out. An American author, writing upon this topic, facetiously remarks:—"The *dam* was built, I don't know when. The Puritans, they say, tried to destroy it—for its *bad name*, perhaps—but could not, because, like a duck, it kept under a high flood of water, until the Cavaliers, making a rush to save it, spiked their guns."

Wending our way to the eastward, we have before us a long and interesting stretch of the meandering Dee, crossed at some distance away by a chaste, yet gossamer-looking bridge, erected in 1852, by Enoch Gerrard, Esq., the projector and proprietor of QUEEN'S PARK, that beautiful range of building land on the opposite side of the river. Those steps on the right, leading down to the river side, are usually known as the *Recorder's Steps*, from their having been erected in 1700, for the accommodation of Roger Comberbach, Esq., then Recorder of Chester.

The Walls here run at a great height above the roadway, until we turn quick round to the northward, at a lofty flight of steps, called the WISHING STEPS. And why the *Wishing Steps*, you ask? Listen, and you shall hear. There's a small bit of "folk lore" bound up with these Steps, and we never pass by them without recalling to mind our boyhood's attempts to master the difficulty. We were always told when a child, and we heartily believe it as a man, that whosoever shall stand at the foot of these steps, and *wish* for any mundane blessing—be it the gold of Ophir, aye, or even Paradise itself—and (mind this!) run up to the head, down to the bottom, and up again to the top of these steps, without taking breath, shall have his fondest wish fulfilled, though it were to the half of the kingdom! The secret is, that no one could possibly accomplish the feat without taking breath some half dozen times.

From the top of the Wishing Steps we have a beautiful prospect of the banks of the Dee, and of the south-eastern environs of the city. From an altitude of some sixty feet, we see beneath us the stream of Deva in all but repose, for above the Causeway the River assumes almost the smoothness of a lake. The iron SUSPENSION BRIDGE, which crosses it midway, and unites the city with its handsome suburb, QUEEN'S PARK, forms a pretty object in the landscape. Though of such spider-like construction, its capabilities and strength have been fully tested. Mr. Dredge, upon whose patent principle the bridge was erected, thus describes it:—"The Queen's Park Bridge is 262 feet span, and 417 long, resting upon massive block masonry (about 3000 cubical feet), which is all below the surface as foundation, and upon it, on each side of the river, is a cluster of four cast-iron pillars, about 33 feet high. The bridge is 23 feet above the ordinary level of the river, and altogether it consists of about 50 tons of iron, the whole of which was wrought on the ground, and the bridge finished in about three months. Its cost was 850*l*." When Mr. Gerrard first projected the Queen's Park, he saw at once the necessity of providing a shorter and better pathway to the city than the old route through Handbridge, and the erection of Queen's Park Suspension Bridge was therefore the starting point of his building operations. Nor has the result belied his confident anticipations of the popularity of the Park; for what was, but a year or two ago, a modest agricultural farm, is now fast developing into an important and delightful suburb. In fact, the salubrity of the air, and the high commanding situation of Queen's Park, together with its beautiful river scenery, and its close proximity to the city, combine to render it peculiarly suitable for villa residences.

Queen's Park and River, from the Wishing Steps.

To our left are some handsome houses, overlooking the river; and behind them, the lofty steeple of ST. JOHN'S CHURCH attracts our especial notice and admiration. This Church is one of our many Chester lions; but, as we shall have to deal with it more at large by and bye, we will pass on now, between some obtrusive houses blocking up the view on one side, and most prolific gardens and orchards on the other, until we reach some modern steps on our left, leading down to the NEWGATE.

This Gate, or its predecessor, was called *Wolfeld* or *Wolfgate*, as also *Pepper Gate*, from its standing at the bottom of the Pepper Street. Tradition informs us that this Gate was "of old time closed up and shut, because a young man stole away a Mayor of Chester's daughter through the same Gate, as she was playing at ball with other maidens in the Pepper Street." Albert Smith, in his "Struggles and Adventures of Christopher Tadpole," perpetuates this tradition, in his own happy and humorous style. *There* 'all who run may read' of the sinful conduct of that wicked young man, and of that almost as froward and faulty young maiden, whose mutual frailties gave birth to the Cheshire proverb, "When the daughter is stolen, shut the Pepper Gate,"—another version of "When the steed is stolen, lock the stable door."

Two or three paces onwards bring us to some pretty little gardens on one side, and on the other to the remains of an old turret, formerly known as *Thimbleby's Tower*, though why or wherefore so designated is, 'in these latter days,' a mystery. Beyond this is a flight of steps, leading down to the WESLEYAN METHODIST CHAPEL, a commodious structure erected in 1811, the principal front of which is towards St. John's Street; to the left of it is the School-room of the same religious community. Within a short distance from this, we mount some half dozen steps, and find ourselves on the top of the EAST GATE, and enjoying a view of the principal Street of the city, at an altitude of some forty feet. At our back is Foregate Street, the old-fashioned mail-coach road to Birmingham and London; while in front we have Eastgate Street, the Cross, and St. Peter's Church, which will receive more particular attention in our next chapter.

Stepping down from the Eastgate on its opposite side, we have now completed our circuit of the Walls; and our appetite being somewhat sharpened by our long walk, we will turn into the "Blossoms," and discuss the merits of such "savoury meats" as "mine host of that ilk" is enabled to lay before us.

CHAPTER V.

The Streets of Chester.—Eastgate Street and Royal Hotel.—The Ancient Rows of Chester.—An American's "notion" of them.—The Architecture of the Rows and Streets.—The High Cross.—The Pentice and Conduit.—The City Bullbait.—St. Peter's Church.

> Let us move slowly through the street,
>   Filled with an ever shifting train,
> Amid the sound of steps that beat
>   The murmuring walks like autumn rain.—BRYANT.

HAVING adequately "refreshed the inner man," we will now, like Don Quixote, sally forth into the STREET "in search of the picturesque," and doubtless we shall there find much of a nature to interest and delight us.

The EASTGATE, under which we are now passing, marks the termination of the old Watling Street,—the line of which is here taken up by the chief of the four great Streets of the city, as planned and excavated by the soldier colonists of once mighty Rome. We have passed from Foregate into EASTGATE STREET, ever the *via principalis* of Chester, and still maintaining that ancient prerogative despite the revolutionary inroads of steam. It is the one great highway for all passengers and conveyances to and from the Station, and as a necessary consequence holds the proud distinction of being, for all business purposes, the main Street of the city.

This arcade on our left is the *Royal Hotel Row*, and the massive pile of buildings of which it forms a part, and from which it derives its name, is the ROYAL HOTEL. The "Royal" is pre-eminently the chief Hotel of the city; for besides being the most central and commodious, it is at the same time *par excellence* the first and most fashionable of all our Chester Hotels, and under its present efficient management, is certainly not surpassed by any similar provincial establishment. Its capacious *Assembly Room* is, with perhaps one exception, the finest room the city can boast, and is consequently in high repute for all literary and musical entertainments. The Royal Hotel enjoys the singular felicity of being *in three distinct parishes*; thus, in a religious, as well as a commercial point of view, "it stands well!"

Royal Hotel.

If you have any curiosity for modern ruins, turn up this passage in front of the Hotel, and see the baneful effects of a chancery suit on what was once a flourishing mart of commerce; and as you look upon that half roofless, tottering fabric, still known as the *Manchester Hall*, "thank your propitious stars" that you, at least, are free from the trammels of the law.

The street immediately beyond on the left, is NEWGATE STREET, anciently styled *Fleshmonger Lane*, from its having been at one time the chief place of business of the butchers. Nearly opposite to it, on the right hand, is ST. WERBURGH STREET, which we shall notice by and bye, when we pay our visit to the Cathedral.

And here we are introduced to another unique characteristic of old Chester,—its venerable Rows. To account satisfactorily for the origin of these Rows, is a problem which has troubled far brighter heads than ours; and, indeed, all we know in the present day is, that in reality we *know nothing* of their earliest history. Some writers, with exuberant fancies, have attributed to the Rows a British foundation: while others, with greater apparent reason, consider them a vestige of the dominion of Rome, and to have been by them erected, conjointly for the purposes of recreation and defence. There are many circumstances which seem to justify this view of the case; particularly that of their resemblance to the porticoes or *vestibula* spoken of by Plautus and other Latin authors. Further confirmatory of their Roman origin, we may add that there is, or was, a street in old Rome, bearing a close analogy to the Rows of Chester. Taking into account also that a Roman Bath and Lavatory exist to this very hour under one of these

Rows, the arguments in favour of their Roman creation are certainly entitled to a fair amount of weight.

If it be difficult to arrive at the early history of these Rows, equally difficult is it to attempt to describe them to a stranger. Distrusting our own powers, we will call in the aid of our friend Albert Smith, who in describing the Rows of what he calls "this marvellous city," proceeds to say that "the passenger's footway lies right through the first floor fronts of the houses—which are cleared away altogether, and above the shop, of ordinary normal position, by the road-side; and thus, the back drawing-rooms, or whatever else they may be, are turned into more shops; and great is the puzzle of the stranger as to whether the roadway is down in the cellar, or he is up stairs on the landing, or the house has turned itself out of window; affording a literal proof of that curious state of domestic affairs so often spoken of. And first he fancies the 'Row'—as it is termed—is like the Quadrant, with the road excavated a floor lower, and shops made under the pavement; and then it reminds him of a Thames-side tavern, with all the shutter wainscots, that divide the large convivial room into so many little philandering ones, drawn away, and the windows knocked out. And finally he arrives at the conclusion that there is nothing else in the world at all like it, except the prints published by the enterprising booksellers who live there. But very convenient is this arrangement for old ladies of weak minds who quail at meeting cattle; and young ladies of extravagant ones who doat on shopping, in spite of the weather. For it raises the first above suspicion even of danger; and shelters the second from being favoured with the visits of the clouds, who cannot here drop in upon them."

Another description from the pen of an American, is still more intelligible. Writing to a friend on the other side of the Atlantic, he says, "The second story of most of the houses is thrown forward, as you have seen it in the old settlers' houses at home. Sometimes it projects several feet, and is supported by posts in the sidewalk. Soon this becomes a frequent and then a continuous arrangement; the posts are generally of stone, forming an arcade,—and you walk beneath them in the shade. Sometimes, instead of posts, a solid wall supports the house above. You observe, as would be likely in an old city, that the surface is irregular, that we are ascending a slight elevation. Notwithstanding the old structure overhead, and the well-worn flagging under foot, we notice the shop fronts are filled with plate-glass, and with all the brilliancy of the most modern art and taste. Turning, to make the contrast more striking, by looking at the little windows and rude carvings of the houses opposite, we see a banister or handrail separates the side-walk from the carriage way, and are astonished, in stepping out to it, to find the street is some ten feet below us. We are evidently on the second floor of the houses. Finding steps leading down we descend into the street, and discover another tier of shops, on the roofs of which we have been walking."

And now for our own brief sketch of the Streets and Rows. This house, near by, with the eccentric gable, and grotesquely carved front is the notable establishment of Messrs. Platt and Son, chemists. The shop itself, which is one of the most chaste and elegant in the city, deserves something more than a mere passing notice, and is worthy the careful inspection of every true 'lover of the beautiful.' "This shop," says the *Chester Courant*, "exhibits one of the most perfect and beautiful examples of the application of architectural and artistic skill and taste to the purposes of business, that we have lately witnessed. It is the joint work of Mr. Penson and Mr. J. Morris, whose combined talents in the constructive and decorative departments, have produced a most successful and elegant illustration of the manner in which the antique character of our domestic architecture can be preserved, with every regard for modern requirements and comforts. The wood-work has been well executed by Mr. Hankey; the floor is paved with fancy tiles from the celebrated manufactory of Messrs. Minton, in Staffordshire; and all the details and fittings of the establishment have been carried out with characteristic taste and propriety. We should hope that the good sense and intelligence, as well as public spirit, displayed by Mr. Platt in this judicious work of restoration, will give an impulse to other improvements in the right direction; while at the same time it excites a regret that alterations have been previously effected, in such utter disregard of the architecture of the Rows, seeing how beautifully their original appearance might have been preserved, to maintain the unique characteristic of the old city." The hope indulged in this last paragraph has not "wasted its fragrance on the desert air," as two neighbouring erections sufficiently testify.

Eastgate Row – Platt and Son, Chemists.

Next door to Messrs. Platt's, and half hidden by the shop which obstructs it just in front, is that favourite resort of the fair sex, the drapery establishment of the Messrs. McLellan. A few yards farther up the street, our eye rests on the gabled *façade*, and handsome shop front of Mr. Bolland, Confectioner, Bride Cake Manufacturer to her Majesty the Queen. What! you are about to get married, are you? Well then, "a word to the wise is sufficient for them,"—give an order to Mr. Bolland for a Chester Bride Cake, and tell him it must be of the quality once supplied to Queen Victoria, and you'll never forget this "sweet and luscious reminiscence" of your approaching wedding-day.

Eastgate Row—Mr. Bolland, Confectioner.

Eastgate Street, North Side.

You will perceive that there is a covered Row also on the other side of this street, similar in character, though not in adornment, to the one we have just been noticing. This is popularly known as the *Pepper Alley Row*, a quaint but gloomy looking region, rendered still more so by the projecting block of buildings displayed in our engraving. Here are the well known drapery establishments of Messrs. Oakes, and Ambrose Williams, and that curious old zigzag erection, occupied by Mr. Hill, Chester's enterprising bootmaker: behind which premises *Pepper Alley Row* "worms its darksome way" into Northgate Street. In this Row are the rooms of the *Church of England Educational Institute,* and the Chester EXCISE OFFICE.

On the ground floor of Messrs. Prichard and Dodd's carpet warehouse in Eastgate Street, there is a curious and interesting old crypt, erected, it is supposed, in the eighth century, an illustration of which will be found in our advertising sheet.

We are now fairly arrived at the HIGH CROSS, and close to the spot where that sacred emblem of the faith in old time stood. This ancient landmark, which was of stone, and elaborately carved, had for centuries ornamented this part of the city, and was a relic much and deservedly prized by the citizens. The Puritans, however, on obtaining possession of the city in 1646, with their characteristic abhorrence of the beautiful, and in direct breach of the articles of surrender, demolished this "fayre crosse." "No cross, no crown" was, in a perverted sense, the motto of these fanatics, whose "organs of destructiveness" must, beyond doubt, have been largely developed. Some fragments of the Cross were picked up at the time, and hidden within the porch of St. Peter's Church hard by, where a century or so afterwards they were discovered, and now ornament the grounds of Netherlegh House, near this city.

Near the Cross was the CONDUIT, to which water was of old brought in pipes to this city from St. Giles' Well in Boughton, and this conduit it was that, according to ancient records, was made to "run with wine" on all public and festive occasions. Here also, upon the south side of St. Peter's Church, was the Penthouse or *Pentice* of the city, where the mayor and magistrates of the old regime sat to administer justice with the one hand, and feed on turtle with the other. A *lean* alderman was as great a curiosity in those days, as a *fat* parish pauper would be deemed in the present. The Pentice, which, with its accessories the Stocks and the Pillory, had too long obstructed this quarter of the city, was pulled down in 1803, and its jurisdiction removed to a more commodious room in the north end of the Exchange.

This locality, crowded as it must have been before the removal of these obstructions, was also annually the scene of the *Corporation Bullbait,* thus vividly described by Cowdroy, a local scribe of the last century: "The Cross is famous for being the annual scene of exhibition of that *polite play* called a bull-bait; where four or five of these *horned heroes* are attended by several hundred lovers of that *rational amusement.* Till within a few years the *dramatis personæ* of this *elegant scene* included even magistracy itself, the mayor and corporation attending in their official habiliments, at the Pentice windows, not only to countenance the *diversions* of the *ring*, but to participate in a sight of its *enjoyments*. A proclamation was also made by the crier of the court, with all the gravity and solemnity of an oration before a *Romish sacrifice*; the elegant composition of which runs thus, 'O*yez*! O*yez*! O*yez*! *If any man stands within twenty yards of the bull-ring, let him take—what comes.*' After which followed the usual public ejaculations, for the safety of the king, and the mayor of the city;" when the *beauties* of the scene commenced, and the dogs immediately *fell to*. Here a prayer for his worship was not unseasonable, as even the ermined cloak was no security against the carcases of dead animals, with which spectators, without distinction, were occasionally saluted. In many ancient boroughs a law formerly prevailed, that no bulls should be slaughtered for food without having been first thus baited by dogs. They loved tender beefsteaks in those days!

This barbarous recreation of a bygone age has long since been put down by the strong arm of the law, and we can now from the very spot study the character of yonder Row, which commanded in those days so near a view of the revolting spectacle.

The ancient and the modern in domestic architecture here stand forth in curious juxtaposition. To the left rests a building of venerable mien, the builder of which flourished probably in the sixteenth century, when Harry the Eighth or Elizabeth swayed the sceptre of England, and when wood and plaster was the chief ingredient in houses of this description.

In the centre of our view, looking affably down on its two-gabled neighbour, is a bold and substantial building of white freestone, erected in 1837, on the site of an older and more picturesque house. This is the business retreat of *our publisher*, and by the same token the oldest book establishment in the city. Here are procurable, in almost endless variety, Guides to Chester and North Wales, local prints, books of views, &c. to suit every imaginable taste and requirement. Perhaps no city in the empire has been so fully and faithfully illustrated as Chester,—Prout, Cuitt, Pickering, Sumners, and others equally celebrated in the walks of art, have plied their pencils in its honour, while the genius of the engraver and the enterprise of the publisher have given permanence to their works.

The other house depicted upon the right of our view, its front bearing the arms of the Apothecaries' Company, is the well-known establishment of MR. J. D. FARRER, Chemist. "Farrer's Cestrian Bouquet" and "Floral Extract" are perfumes too well known to the fair *élite* of Chester to need more than a passing notice here. Strangers and visitors, however, will thank us for the hint that these, and other like gems of the toilet, fragrant mementos of "rare old Chester," are "prepared and sold only by Mr. Farrer."

East Gate Row.

Opposite to these premises stands the parish CHURCH OF ST. PETER, the site of which is supposed to have been also that of the Roman *Prætorium*. Tradition ascribes the first building of this church to that Mercian celebrity, the Countess Ethelfleda, who raised an edifice in the centre of the city to the mutual honour of St. Peter and St. Paul. These two saints had, up to that time, presided over the destinies of the mother church of Chester, now the Cathedral, but a 'new light' having sprung up in the person of the virgin-wife, St. Werburgh, the two aforesaid apostles were relieved of their charge, and a new Church erected and dedicated to them on the spot we are now surveying. Bradshaw the monk, from whose quaint historic poem we have already quoted, thus records the translation:—

> And the olde churche of Peter and of Paule
>   By a generall counsell of the spiritualte,
> With helpe of the Duke moost principall,
>   Was translate to the myddes of the sayd cite,
>   Where a paresshe churche was edified truele
> In honour of the aforesaid apostoles twayne,
> Whiche shall for ever by grace divine remayne.

St. Paul's connection with the church appears to have ceased before the Conquest, since which time the edifice has been once or twice rebuilt. The spire is recorded to have been re-edified in 1479, in which year the *parson of the parish*, with his officers, ate a goose upon the top, and cast the well-picked bones into the four streets below. The ecclesiastics of those days were a jovial crew,—none of your lean, skewery-built men, like their degenerate types of the present day,—but priests of size and substance; men who quaffed their wine and sack right merrily; and who evidently looked after the *spirits* of their flocks more than after their souls. Must not those have been "good old times!" The east and part of the south sides of the church were rebuilt in 1640, just before the breaking out of the great Civil War. The "parson and goose spire" having been injured by lightning in 1780, was that same year removed. The present square steeple was rebuilt in 1813; and the illuminated clock which ornaments the south front was first publicly lit up in 1835. The interior of the church, which contains some venerable monuments, has of late years been considerably improved and beautified.

CHAPTER VI.

Watergate Street.—God's Providence House.—Bishop Lloyd's House.—The Puppet Show Explosion.—Trinity Church.—Dean Swift and the Yacht,—St. Martin's and St. Bridget's Churches.—The Stanley Palace.—Watergate.—Port of Chester.

WESTWARD, ho! a few steps, and we find ourselves moving along Watergate Street; once, and when Chester was a thriving port, the chief street of the city. As with men, so

> There is a tide in the affairs of *streets*,
> Which taken at the flood, leads on to fortune;

but the tide for Watergate Street has ebbed away, and now flows in other and more favoured channels. Still, as we shall presently see, this Street is not behind any of its neighbours in absorbing interest. You will perceive that, like Eastgate Street, it has the Cestrian characteristic on either side,—its high-level Row. The one upon the right hand, adjoining St. Peter's Church, is, perhaps, as good a specimen as we have now left to us of the "Rows" of the last century. Had we the time to spare, a ramble along this Row, and a hole-and-corner visit to the numerous alleys that intersect it, would convince the most sceptical that there is more in Chester than meets the eye. But we must away,—for see! here is an odd-looking tenement, on the other side the street, inviting our attention. Two hundred years ago that house was in the pride of youth, and the residence of a family of "some rank and standing," as is evidenced by the armorial bearings carved on one of the beams; but, as somebody or other (Longfellow, we believe), has justly enough observed, "it is not always May!", in proof of which this house has of late years been occupied as a sausage shop, and now shelters the defenceless head of a barber. Small and low are the rooms of this house—absurdly so to the critic of the present generation; and so contracted is the ceiling of the Row at this point, that no man of ordinary stature can pass along without stooping. Is it not a quaint old spot? Look up at yon inscription on the cross-beam. Tradition avers that this house was the only one in the city that escaped the plague, which ravaged the city during the seventeenth century. In gratitude for that deliverance, the owner of the house is said to have carved upon the front the words we are now reading—

1652. GOD'S PROVIDENCE IS MINE INHERITANCE. 1652.

God's Providence House, Water Gate Street.

On the right hand, lower down, is GOSS STREET; and still lower, CROOK STREET, both destitute of interest to sight-seers: but, exactly opposite to Crook Street, stand three fine gable-fronted houses, the centre one of which deserves our attention and admiration. This house is, without exception, the most curious and remarkable of its kind in Chester, and one which, perhaps, has no parallel in Great Britain. Prout has immortalised it in one of his inimitable sketches, of which the accompanying woodcut is a reduced, yet faithful copy. The origin of the house seems to be lost in fable; but, in the present day, it is usually styled BISHOP LLOYD'S HOUSE, from the fact of that Cestrian prelate dying about the date (1615,) carved on one of the panels, and from certain coats-of-arms which decorate the front, bearing some analogy to the bearings of his family. Grotesquely carved from the apex of the gable to the very level of the Row, this house exhibits a profusion of ornament, and an eccentricity of design, unattempted in any structure of the kind within our knowledge. It is, indeed, a unique and magnificent work of art. To say nothing of the designs in the higher compartments, it must suffice here to state, that the subjects of the lower panels lay the plan of human redemption prominently before the eye. In the first panel, we have Adam and Eve in Paradise, in a state of sinless nudity; then comes the first great consequence of the Fall, Cain murdering Abel his brother. To this follows Abraham offering up his Son Isaac; typical of the "one great Sacrifice for us all." The seventh compartment has a curious representation of the Immaculate Conception, whereby "Christ Jesus came into the world to save sinners." Ridiculous have been some of the attempts of "Local Guide-makers" to arrive at the real meaning of this design: some have gravely set it down as the "Flight into Egypt;" while another and later "unfortunate" has sapiently pronounced it to be "Susannah and the Elders." The eighth panel symbolises the completion of the great sacrifice, the Crucifixion of Christ, in Simeon's prophecy to the Virgin,—"Yea, a sword shall pierce through thine own heart also." The three centre compartments contain the arms of the reigning monarch, James I., England's Solomon, as he was called,—the supposed arms and quarterings of Bishop Lloyd,—and a Latin inscription, with the date 1615. If it be true that

>A thing of beauty is a joy for ever,

then will this house, as a masterpiece of art, be an object of interest and delight to strangers, "till time itself shall be no more." We should step up into the Row at this point, and scrutinise the indescribable forms of men and beasts which ornament and support the oaken pillars in front.

Bishop Lloyd's House, Water Gate Row.

A few steps lower down the Row is a passage or alley, communicating with Commonhall Street, called *Puppet Show Entry*. This passage is chiefly memorable as the scene of a most terrific explosion, which shook the city like an earthquake, on the anniversary of the Gunpowder Plot, November 5th, 1772. A large room in this passage was fitted up as a sort of Marionette Theatre,—a large audience had assembled,—the puppets were going through their strange evolutions,—when, by some appalling misfortune, eight hundred-weight of gunpowder lodged in a warehouse below suddenly blew up with a tremendous report, killing the showman and twenty-two others; eighty-three, besides, being more or less seriously injured. In remembrance of that fearful calamity, this alley has been ever since known as the *Puppet Show Entry*.

Where that new range of superior houses now stands, on the opposite side of the street, was, until very recently, a fine old mansion of wood and plaster, the city residence of the Mainwarings, a notable Cheshire family.

Just below we have, upon the left hand, WEAVER STREET, anciently *St. Alban's Lane*, leading to the spot where the Church and *Monastery of the White Friars* in times past stood. Of this monastic establishment no vestige remains, except a portion of the western wall, which is still visible from Weaver Street. The spire of this Church, which was of noble dimensions, served mariners as a landmark in steering their vessels up to the Walls of Chester.

On the right side of Watergate Street is TRINITY STREET, in which is the oldest dissenting chapel in the city. It was erected in 1700, by the followers and friends of MATTHEW HENRY, the nonconformist, a learned and earnest preacher of his day, and author of the celebrated "Commentary on the Holy Scriptures" which bears his name.

Passing Trinity Street, we arrive at the Parish CHURCH of the HOLY AND UNDIVIDED TRINITY, the first foundation of which is lost in remote obscurity. So early as the year 1188, we find Walter, rector of this Church, witnessing a deed relating to the Church of Rostherne, in this county. Very little, if any, of the original Church now exists; the west side is, perhaps, the most ancient portion of the structure, as it at present stands. Prior to 1811, the steeple was surmounted by a handsome spire, which, proving on examination to be in a dilapidated state, was pulled down, and the present square tower substituted. The reason for this change is not very obvious; perhaps there may have been bickerings and dissensions in the vestry as to the relative cost of the two, and the authorities thought it best to give up the *point*, in order to make matters *square*. The advowson of the Church is vested in the Earl of Derby, having previously belonged to the Norman barony of Montalt, one of the titles created by Hugh Lupus, Earl of Chester.

The interior is worthy the inspection of the curious. Near the south-west entrance is the baptismal font, by the side of which lies the defaced effigy of a mail-clad knight, Sir John Whitmore by name, representative in the reign of Edward III. of the Whitmores of Thurstaston, a Cheshire family of knightly lineage and renown. This monument was discovered in 1853, under a pew at the south-west end; the face, hands, and knees, having been barbarously cut away, to suit the flooring of the pew. In its perfect state, the monument must have been one of the purest symmetry and beauty, and was evidently the work of an eminent sculptor, the Westmacott or Gibson of his day. The legend runs thus:—

> Hic jacet Ioannes de Whitmore, qui obiit 3 kal. Octob. A.D. 1374.

A brass plate on the south side of the altar commemorates the burial of MATTHEW HENRY, June 22nd, 1714. He who had during life been a rigid nonconformist, at the "last sad scene of all" conformed to the faith of his forefathers, and lies interred in the chancel of that parish in which he had so long ministered as a dissenter.

The bones of another celebrity "lie mouldering here,"—Dr. Parnell, the poet, Archdeacon of Clogher, who was buried in this Church, October 23, 1718. Other monuments of interest ornament (or shall we rather say *deface?*) the pillars and chancel walls. In one of the western windows are some remnants of ancient stained glass, and an obituary memorial, of chaste design, has of late years been put up in one of the small east windows of St. Patrick's aisle.

A good view of Trinity Church is obtained from the end of Nicholas Street, just opposite to that ancient hostelry, the YACHT INN. The YACHT is, without exception, the most picturesque and curious of all our Chester inns. Time was when it was the first hotel of the city, and even now, "grown grey with long and faithful service," lacks nothing that can render it a fit home for the wayfarer, whom chance or design has brought to the old city. Americans, who lust after the ancient and venerable, and who delight in the rare timber houses of old England, will do well to select snug apartments at the *Yacht*, for its host, Mr. White, is the very impersonation of a true British Boniface. But the *Yacht*, apart altogether from the qualities of "mine host," and his well-filled cellar of "Huxley's Fine," has other claims upon our attention. It was at this house, then in the zenith of its glory, that the eccentric and witty Dean Swift (who has not read his "Gulliver's Travels?") stayed, on one of his journeys into Ireland. The Dean, being of a convivial turn, invited the dignitaries of the Cathedral to a supper at the *Yacht*, but to his great mortification not one of them appeared. Disgusted at this return to his hospitality, the Dean scratched with his diamond ring on one of the windows of this house the following distich, not over complimentary to the church or the city,—

> Rotten without and mouldering within,
> This place and its clergy are both near akin!

So much for the *Yacht*. The CUSTOM HOUSE, immediately opposite, with its low stuccoed front, has nothing to arrest the special notice of visitors.

Trinity Church, Yacht Inn, and Custom House.

NICHOLAS STREET, which branches off in a direct line towards the Castle, has on the right hand a terrace of well-built, first-class houses, extending as far as the corner of *Grey Friars*. From the circumstance of every alternate house in this terrace being occupied by a doctor, it has latterly acquired the appropriate cognomen of *Pill-box Promenade*!

Some distance up Nicholas Street, on the left hand, is ST. MARTIN'S CHURCH, a humble brick building, erected in 1721, in the place of an older structure dating back to the thirteenth century. St. Martin's parish has recently been united to that of St. Bridget, and the services of this Church are now, in consequence, discontinued.

Moving along *St. Martin's Ash*, as this locality is termed, past *Cuppin Street*, where the Old Gas Works are situate, we obtain a good front view of the new Church of ST. BRIDGET. This Church, or rather its predecessor, stood originally at the other end of GROSVENOR STREET, immediately opposite to St. Michael's Church, and its foundation has been by some ascribed to Offa, King of Mercia, in the eighth century. Be this as it may, there are records preserved which establish its existence at least as early as the year

1200. On the erection of the *Grosvenor Bridge*, it was found that this Church stood exactly in the track of the projected New Road, now called GROSVENOR STREET, and an act of parliament was consequently obtained for its removal. The old Church was demolished in 1827, and the gravestones and bodies removed, where practicable, to the new burial-ground adjoining the present Church. The first stone of the new edifice was laid October 12, 1827, by Dr. C. J. Blomfield, the present Bishop of London, who at that time presided over the see of Chester. This structure presents outwardly none of the characteristics of a Christian Church; and might easily be mistaken for some pagan temple, rather than for one dedicated to the worship of the Most High.

Returning to Watergate Street, we see before us LINEN HALL STREET, called formerly *Lower Lane*, from its being at one time the last street on this side of the city. There is nothing to interest us in this street, which terminates with *St. Martin's in the Fields*, at the rear of the Gaol, and General Infirmary. So late as the sixteenth century, there was at the further end of this street an ancient Church, quoted in old deeds as the *Church of St. Chad*, but the place thereof is now nowhere to be found.

Lower still down Watergate Street, is LINEN HALL PLACE, where the Chester CHESS CLUB holds its meetings, and where players of every country and clime are sure of a hearty and welcome reception.

Nearly opposite to this Place, up a narrow, inconvenient passage, is a house which invites and eminently deserves our notice and admiration. This house is styled indifferently the OLD PALACE, and STANLEY HOUSE, from its having been originally the city palace or residence of the Stanleys of Alderley, a family of note in the county, and now ennobled. This is an elaborately carved, three-gabled house, and is perhaps the oldest unmutilated specimen of a timber house remaining in the city, the date of its erection being carved on the front,—1591. The sombre dignity of its exterior pervades also the internal construction of this house,—the large rooms, the panelled walls, the oaken floors, the massive staircase, all pointing it out as the abode of aristocracy in the olden time.

The Old Palace, or Stanley House.

From hence to the WATERGATE is little more than a stone's throw; but on the left is the handsome city residence of H. Potts, Esq., representative of a family long and honourably connected with the county. This house and the locality round occupy the site of the ancient *Monastery of the Black Friars*, where the black-cowled faithful 'fasted and prayed' down to the period of the Dissolution, but of which scarcely any traces, save the fragment of a wall, are now discernible.

The passage to the right leads to STANLEY PLACE, near which, in 1779, a Roman Hypocaust, and the remains of a house, also of the same remote period, were discovered. Such portions of these remains as escaped the ruthless pickaxes of the workmen, were removed to Oulton Park, and now ornament the museum of its present worthy owner, Sir P. Grey Egerton, Bart., M.P. for the county.

Beyond the Watergate are PARADISE ROW, overlooking the ROODEYE,— and the two CRANE STREETS; beyond which we are introduced to that fabulous existence of modern days,—the PORT of Chester. Time was when we might have tuned our harps to a different key, but now, alas! we can only lament the fallen condition of our ancient port, and the wretched indifference of those 'high in authority,' who by their senseless apathy in past days have brought the maritime trade of Chester to its present lifeless and ignominious state. This is a sore subject; so we will at once retrace our steps to the Cross, and in the next chapter continue our perambulations through the city.

CHAPTER VII.

Bridge Street.—Ancient Crypt.—The Blue Posts and the Knave of Clubs.—Roman Bath.—Grosvenor Street.—New Savings Bank.—The Cemetery.—Curzon Park and Hough Green.—The Port of Saltney.—St. Michael's Church.—St. Olave's Church.—The Gamull House.—St. Mary's Church.

HEIGHO! After our bootless lamentation over the deceased Port of Chester, it is refreshing to return once more to an atmosphere of life and activity.

Turning our faces towards the south, we have before us BRIDGE STREET, another of the four great Roman roads of the city. Here again we see the Rows,—those strange old Rows!—threading their tubelike course along both sides of the Street. The one upon the right hand is called the *Scotch Row*, from the merchants north of the Tweed 'clanning' together there, during the two great FAIRS, held annually at Chester from time immemorial. It should be remembered that, except at these privileged times, none but freemen were permitted to trade within the city; whence is to be attributed the large concourse of foreign tradesmen to these once important Fairs. Since the downfall of this monopoly, the *Scotch Row* has become a desert wilderness, so far as business is concerned; but it will still serve as an admirable index to the stranger of what the Rows of Chester were a hundred years ago. The street fronts of the houses in this Row are more than ordinarily diversified,—the square red brick, the everlasting gable of every shape and size, the stately bow-window, and the ponderous, overhanging Dutch fronts, all flaunting their pretensions within this circumscribed space. Previous to 1839, no special archæological interest attached to this locality; but in that year while excavating for a warehouse behind the shop of Messrs. Powell and Edwards, cutlers, a discovery was made which at once set all the antiquaries of Chester "by the ears." The late Rev. J. Eaton, Precentor of the Cathedral, an architectural authority in his day, made the following Report upon this ANCIENT CRYPT, as it is called, for the use of the proprietors. To these gentlemen, and particularly to Mr. Edwards, the representative of the firm, the public are deeply indebted for their intelligence and courtesy, in not only preserving intact this relic of the past, but also for so readily affording admission to the structure:—

> "The lower parts of several of the houses in the four principal streets of Chester exhibit indubitable signs that they have been built on the remains of the religious

- 54 -

buildings with which, prior to the Reformation, this city abounded.

"The ancient Crypt discovered by Messrs. Powell and Edwards is of an oblong form, running from east to west. The following are its dimensions, viz. length, forty-two feet; breadth, fifteen feet three inches; height, from the surface of the floor to the intersection of the groinings of the roof, fourteen feet. This Crypt was partially lighted through the upper part of the west end, in which there are three small windows, divided by stone mullions, and protected by iron bars. The upper part of the groining on the centre window appears to have been cut away to admit of more light. On examining the intersection of the groins, marks were discovered from the lead on the stone-work, that a couple of lamps had been used for lighting. The entrance to the east end is by a flight of steps cut out of the rock to the height of three feet. On the south side is an Anglo-Norman-Gothic doorway, which is attained by three or four semicircular steps, and forms an outlet within its inner and outer wall by another flight of steps to the surface above the building. In a niche on the south side of the window is a font in excellent preservation.

"The architecture is Anglo-Norman-Gothic, and the groins are of the third class of groining, which came into common use about the year 1180, and was succeeded in the next class of groins in the year 1280, so that if we date this roof as being erected about the year 1230, we shall not be far from the era of its real construction."

Messrs. Powell and Edwards make no charge for admission: we must not omit, therefore, ere we pass out from the *Crypt*, to drop a stray piece of silver into the hat of the *Blue Coat Boy* who stands modestly at the door. Charity is seldom ill-bestowed; but here we have the special privilege of contributing, in however slight a degree, to the gratuitous education of the orphan and the friendless.

The Row upon the left hand is the one most frequented, forming a junction at right angles with Eastgate Row, before described. In the sixteenth century this Row was distinguished by the name of the *Mercers' Row*, from the predominance here, probably, of that most enticing class of tradesmen. The love of dress and finery was evidently, even in those days, woman's chief besetting sin!

A little way down this Row was an ancient tavern, called the *Blue Posts*, supposed to be the identical house now occupied by Mr. Brittain, woollendraper. In this house a curious incident is stated to have occurred in 1558, which tradition has handed down to us in the following terms. It appears that—

> "Dr. Henry Cole, Dean of St. Paul's, was charged by Queen Mary with a commission to the council of Ireland, which had for its object the persecution of the Irish protestants. The doctor stopped one night here on his way to Dublin, and put up at the *Blue Posts*, then kept by a Mrs. Mottershead. In this house he was visited by the mayor, to whom, in the course of conversation, he related his errand; in confirmation of which he took from his cloak bag a leather box, exclaiming in a tone of exultation, 'Here is what will lash the heretics of Ireland!' This announcement was caught by the landlady, who had a brother in Dublin: and while the commissioner was escorting his worship down-stairs, the good woman, prompted by an affectionate regard for the safety of her brother, opened the box, took out the commission, and placed in lieu thereof a pack of cards, with the *knave of clubs* uppermost! This the doctor carefully packed up, without suspecting the transformation; nor was the deception discovered till his arrival in the presence of the lord deputy and privy council at the castle of Dublin. The surprise of the whole assembly, on opening the supposed commission, may be more easily imagined than described. The doctor, in short, was immediately sent back for a more satisfactory authority; but, before he could return to Ireland, Queen Mary had breathed her last. It should be added that the ingenuity and affectionate zeal of the landlady were rewarded by Elizabeth with a pension of £40 a-year."

The first street we meet with on the right hand is COMMONHALL STREET, so called from the *Common Hall* of the city having been at one time situate there. This hall of justice stood upon the south side of the street, and close to those venerable-looking almshouses still situate there. It had previously been the *Chapel of St. Ursula*, which was founded there, with an *Hospital* for decayed persons, by Sir Thomas Smith, in 1532. The Hospital of St. Ursula still weathers the storm, in those odd-looking, tottering almshouses on the south side of this street. Lower down Bridge Street, on the same side, is another break in the row, formed by *Pierpoint Lane*, not now a thoroughfare, but through which went a passage in olden time to the *Common Hall*, just referred to.

Scarcely so far down as this last-named lane, and on the opposite side of Bridge Street, is a new and handsome range of buildings, erected in 1853 by Mr. Alderman Royle. On the higher side of these premises, and adjoining the Feathers Hotel, exist a ROMAN HYPOCAUST and *Sweating Bath*, of surpassing interest, and in a state almost as perfect as when first erected. The following account of this "ancient of days" is the result of a recent personal visit to the bath.

It consists of two rooms, considerably below the present level of the street—the first being fifteen feet long, eight feet wide, and about six and a half feet deep. The Hypocaust is of rectangular shape, about the same size, but, except at the entrance, not more than half as deep as the first chamber. It was originally supported by thirty-two square pillars, two and a half feet high, and one foot in diameter at top and bottom: twenty-eight of these pillars still remain. Brick tiles, eighteen inches square, and three inches thick, surmount these pillars; and over these are placed tiles two feet square, perforated here and there with small holes, through which the heat ascended to the *sweating chamber* above. The sweating room, or Sudatory, was immediately over the Hypocaust, and was fitted with seats for the bathers, who soon found themselves in a hot perspiration. They were then scraped carefully with an instrument constructed for the purpose, or else plunged into a cold water bath; after which they were rubbed down with towels, anointed with fresh oil, and then repaired to the tiring room: there they dressed themselves, deposited their *denarii* for the attendants, and then went their way, having enjoyed a luxury which few but Romans had then learned to indulge in.

As we have before stated, the buildings above and around have been only recently rebuilt: but Messrs. Royle, the proprietors, with that antiquarian zeal, and true public spirit, which have ever distinguished them, took especial precautions to preserve, both from injury and molestation, this curious relic of proud old Rome. Since the adjacent premises have been rebuilt, the bath is much easier of access than it was before; and visitors can now inspect these remains without any personal sacrifice, either of cleanliness or comfort.

Lower down than the Roman Bath, there was, until recently, a break in this Row, occasioned by a narrow lane, which leads up to the stables of the Feathers Hotel. This inconvenience has now been obviated by a neat wooden bridge, stretching across the passage from row to row; and we can now walk along, without the slightest obstruction, till we come to St. Michael's Church.

The large and well-conceived street upon the right hand is GROSVENOR STREET, capable, under proper management, of being made the finest street of the city. It is flanked on the right side by WHITE FRIARS, formerly *Foster's Lane*, in which the Church and Monastery of that fraternity was at one time situate.

Grosvenor Street, and King's Head Inn.

At the junction of White Friars with Grosvenor Street stands that capital, well-conducted establishment, the KING'S HEAD INN. This is one of those quiet, cosy-looking houses, in which, the moment a traveller enters, he feels himself "at home;" and certainly, under the presidency of Mr. and Mrs. Bedson, he will find that—"deny it who can!"—domestic comforts are still to be enjoyed in an old English inn.

Some thirty yards up the street, on the right hand, is Cuppin Street, before noticed; and nearly opposite to it, an old and narrow street called *Bunce Lane*, leading off to St. Mary's Church and the Castle. Beyond, upon the same side, is an elegant structure of white freestone, erected in 1853, from the designs of Mr. James Harrison, of this city, to wit, the Chester SAVINGS BANK. The architecture of this building is of the Tudor style; and the genius of Mr. Harrison has accomplished a work which, while highly creditable to himself, is, at the same time, a genuine ornament to the city. The clock turret at the north-west corner, though it somewhat destroys the equilibrium of sight, yet, on the whole, adds much of beauty to the general fabric. The clock, which works four faces, and chimes the quarters on two melodious bells, was constructed by Mr. Joyce, of Whitchurch.

The ordinary business of this Bank is conducted in two large rooms, nearly twenty feet square, on the ground floor; over which a spiral staircase conducts to the committee and lecture-room, a noble apartment, forty-one feet long by twenty feet wide, lit on the north and west sides by four handsome traceried windows. The panelled ceiling, and other internal decorations of this room, are exceedingly chaste, and in happy unison with its exterior character. The Bank was formally transferred here from Goss Street in March, 1853. Here the poor and thrifty hoard up their little savings; the shillings grow into pounds, and provision is thus quietly, but surely, made against the rainy day. Let us never despise the day of small things, remembering that the foundation of many a rich man's fortune has been laid with his first shilling deposited in a Savings Bank.

On the right is St. Bridget's Church; and from this spot we obtain a capital view of the CASTLE, including the Grand Entrance, Shire Hall, Barrack Square, and Julius Cæsar's Tower. We have noticed the Castle more particularly in our "Walk round the City Walls;" so we will now pass on towards the Grosvenor Bridge, one of the modern wonders of old Chester. From the parapet of this bridge we obtain a splendid view of the Roodeye and river, as well as of the Viaduct and Railway Bridge in the distance. This bridge has obtained an unenviable notoriety from its having broken down with a passenger train, on May 24, 1847, precipitating the whole of the carriages and passengers into the river below. By this accident four persons were killed upon the spot, and very many others more or less injured.

We are no sooner over the Grosvenor Bridge than we feel ourselves at once out of range of the town, and breathing the fresh and balmy air of the country. Bowers of trees are on either side of us, through which we can see, upon our left hand, something which seems like unto a Christian temple. The gateway we are approaching stands invitingly open; let us therefore step in, and cast a quiet glance at the prospect around. Despite the rose-clad lodge which guards the entrance, and the numerous flowers and shrubs that everywhere greet the eye, we are at once struck that this is a sacred scene, a royal domain of the grim King Death. "Tread lightly," then, all who would venture in hither, for assuredly "this is holy ground;" and while we reverently scan the numerous memorials of the departed lying scattered around, let us all prepare, ere the day be too far spent, to follow them in peace and in hope to our last earthly home. There are few but have, at some time or other, borne a friend to the grave—perhaps even the soul and centre of their domestic hearth; *our* 'household god' lies peacefully *here*. To all such these lines, coming thus from among the tombs, will lose nought of their original force and beauty:

> Forget not the Dead, who have loved, who have left us,
>   Who bend o'er us now from their bright homes above;

> But believe, never doubt, that the God who bereft us
>   Permits them to mingle with friends they still love.
>
> Repeat their fond words—all their noble deeds cherish—
>   Speak pleasantly of them who left us in tears;
> From our lips their dear names other joys should not perish,
>   While time bears our feet through the valley of years.
>
> Yea, forget not the Dead, who are evermore nigh us,
>   Still floating sometimes round our dream-haunted bed;
> In the loneliest hour, in the crowd they are by us!—
>   Forget not the Dead,—oh! forget not the Dead!

The CHESTER CEMETERY, for such is the beautiful spot we are exploring, seems as if formed by nature for the repose of the dead—all is so still, so serenely still, within its halllowed sphere. Nature and Art have alike combined to produce here a retreat worthy of the dead, and yet full of beauty and allurement for the living; while on the lake below us

> See how yon swans, with snowy pride elate,
> Arch their high necks, and sail along in state;

In fine, the beautiful trees and shrubs, the serpentine walks, the rustic bridges, the isle-dotted lake, the ivied rock-work, the modest chapels, and, above all, the tombstones of chaste and mostly appropriate design which meet us at every turn—all point out the Chester Cemetery as a fitting refuge for all, who in serious mood would "commune with their own hearts, and be still." But we must not longer linger here, save to cast a look towards the ancient city, the river, Castle, and the New and Old Bridges, which from the north side of the Cemetery present to the eye a varied and truly interesting panorama.

Opposite to the Cemetery, reached from the Grosvenor Road by a pretty little suspension bridge, is CURZON PARK, the property of Earl Howe, and upon which some handsome, aristocratic villas have been erected. It is from Curzon Park whence that view of the city is obtained which figures as the frontispiece of this "Guide," and certainly from no point is old Chester seen to greater advantage than from this elevated and commanding locality.

Continuing our course from the Cemetery, we come to what we who live in towns and travel only by rail, so seldom meet with—a turnpike-gate,— through which we see the *Grosvenor Gateway*, to be noticed more particularly hereafter. A road upon the left leads to HANDBRIDGE and QUEEN'S PARK, and that upon the right to one of the most thriving suburbs of Chester, HOUGH GREEN, and SALTNEY. Now, *we* are not troubled with a superfluity of grey hairs, yet do we well remember SALTNEY when but two houses occupied the site of the present little town. There was nothing heard *then* of the *Port* and *trade of Saltney*! But since the cutting of the two great Railways which form a junction, though not an alliance, at this spot, SALTNEY has rapidly risen in importance and population. A large Ironworks and coal trade have been established, new streets have sprung up, yclept severally Cable Street, Curzon Street, Wood Street, &c., and the number of inhabitants is now computed at about 3000. The new Church, erected in 1854–5, comes scarcely within our province, standing just beyond the boundaries of the city, which is here separated only by a narrow lane from the Principality of WALES. Looking at the rapidity with which building is going on at SALTNEY, and at the causes which have induced it, we shall not go far wrong in predicting for this 'child of the old city' a long future of commercial health and prosperity.

Returning once more to BRIDGE STREET, we must pause awhile at ST. MICHAEL'S CHURCH, standing at the north-east angle of this street and Pepper Street. A Church existed here, in connexion with a Monastery of the same name, almost coëval with the Conquest. In the year 1178, John de Lacy, constable of Chester, whose ancestor Roger de Lacy had devised the *Monastery of St. Michael* to the Prior of Norton, gave a messuage adjoining this church to the Abbot of Stanlaw. Two years afterwards, viz., on Mid-lent Sunday 1180, this Church and monastery were, with a large portion of the city, destroyed by fire; and Bradshaw the poet-monk assures us, doubtless "on the best authority," that if it had not been for the virtues attaching to the holy shrine of St. Werburgh, the whole city would have then "lain in dust and ashes!" He that hath faith enough to remove mountains, let him swallow this also—*we* are confessedly an infidel. The *Monastery* does not appear to have been rebuilt after the Great Fire; but of the *Church* frequent mention is made in old charters and deeds. It has been several times rebuilt—the last time in 1849–50—so that it is, at this moment, the newest ecclesiastical edifice in the city. Mr. James Harrison, the architect of the Savings Bank and Music Hall, furnished the plans and elevations for the present Church of St. Michael.

St. Michael's Church, and Lecture Hall.

Perhaps the best view we can have of ST. MICHAEL'S CHURCH is from a little way down Bridge Street, just opposite to that useful building, the NEW LECTURE HALL. Chester has long stood in need of a room for such purposes, moderate in dimensions, and conveniently situate; and Dr. Norton, the proprietor of the new LECTURE HALL, has laudably ministered to that want, by providing a public room admirably adapted, from its size and situation, for popular lectures and musical entertainments. Our illustration embraces a view both of the LECTURE HALL and of ST. MICHAEL'S CHURCH.

Just behind where we have been standing is a curious relic of the timber architecture of Chester—the Falcon Inn. A few yards higher up than the Falcon, the street was for nearly two centuries blocked up by a strange-looking timber building, erected by Randle Holme in 1655, called the OLD LAMB ROW. While this house was in being it was the greatest curiosity of its kind in the city; but in 1821, the decaying timbers suddenly parted from their bearings, and the entire pile fell in with a great crash, to the unspeakable relief of the pent-up thoroughfare, but to the great chagrin and regret of the antiquary.

We are now descending LOWER BRIDGE STREET, which abounds, on either side, with those queer-looking tenements, not to be met with in such numbers and variety in any other city but Chester. Here is one with the date 1603, evidently the residence, in its earliest days, of some Cestrian magnate long since "returned to his dust."

But see! yonder rattles a bus, with a party from the station, down to that first-class establishment, the ALBION HOTEL. This house has no superior in the city; for while of handsome external proportions, its interior arrangements have all been conceived with especial regard to the comfort and convenience of visitors. The *Assembly Room* is the largest in the city; the other rooms are light and lofty; in short, under the zealous superintendence of Mr. and Mrs. Chambers, none who once make acquaintance with the ALBION will ever sigh for better or more comfortable quarters. Behind the HOTEL are extensive pleasure-grounds, as well as a verdant and spacious Bowling-green, to which there is a carriage entrance from *Park Street.*

Only a step or two from the Albion, and on the same side, near the residence of MR. SNAPE, the eminent dentist, is *St. Olave's Lane*, so named from the Lilliputian church, dedicated to that saint, at its south-west corner. This Church dates back earlier than the Conquest. The advowson in the eleventh century was vested in the Botelers or Butlers; from whom it passed by gift of Richard Pincerna, in 1101, to the Abbey of St. Werburgh. ST. OLAVE'S appears to have been always "in low water," a *starving* rather than a *living*; for in 1393, on account of its poverty, the parish was temporarily united with St. Mary's. Down to the seventeenth century, however, it eked out a precarious existence; but after the close of the civil war, the ordinary services of the church were discontinued for about a century; when they were again resumed, until the final extinction of ST. OLAVE'S as a distinct parish, in 1841. In that year the Church was finally closed, and the parish united to that of St. Michael. The "powers that be" are fast allowing this ancient structure to develop into a ruin.

Lower Bridge Street, and Albion Hotel.

Opposite to St. Olave's is CASTLE STREET; beyond which, up a flight of steps, is a large tenement, of late years known as the *Boarding-School Yard.* This was in the seventeenth century the mansion-house of the Gamulls, a worthy Cheshire family; and here, on September 27, 1645, Sir Francis Gamull (Mayor of Chester in 1634) lodged and entertained Charles I. on his

Majesty's visit to Chester during the great Civil War. The house is now divided into tenements; but several of the rooms still retain evidence of their original splendour.

Still farther down, we have upon the left *Duke Street*, and on the right *Shipgate Street*, through which, in old time, the citizens used to pass by way of the Ship Gate, across the river, into Handbridge. It leads also to St. Mary's Hill; on the summit of which, half-embowered in trees, we are introduced to the ancient Church of ST. MARY.

ST. MARY'S CHURCH is in all probability of Norman foundation; and is in old writings termed indifferently *St. Mary's of the Castle*, and *St. Mary's upon the Hill*, to distinguish it from the handsome Church of the White Friars, which was also dedicated to that saint. Randle Gernons, fourth earl of Chester, presented the advowson to the Monastery of St. Werburgh; but shortly after the dissolution it was wrested from the dean and chapter by that rapacious spoiler of churches and religious houses, Sir R. Cotton, who afterwards sold it for 100*l.* to John Brereton of Wettenhall. In this family it continued for about a century, when it passed by purchase to the Wilbrahams of Dorfold. From them it came by marriage to the Hills of Hough, whose representative sold it to the father of the present Marquis of Westminster. Of no external beauty, with a tower of miserably stunted proportions (so built in 1715, in order that it might not overlook the Castle), ST. MARY'S CHURCH is nevertheless well deserving a visit from all lovers of true ecclesiastical order. Here is a Church which, when *we* first remember it, was a disgrace alike to the authorities and to the parish—choked up with galleries of hideous shape and size—disfigured with pews of unsightly construction,—the walls and ceilings buried in plaster, whitewash, and dust, and the monuments and windows all alike in a state of ruin and decay. Let us step into the Church, and survey the change which has been effected within a few short years. We are no sooner inside, than we are at once convinced that this is indeed the House of God, gradually, and, under the auspices of the present worthy rector, *judiciously* returning to its first estate, as a seemly temple, worthy of the Most High. Here is none of that venerable dust, that insidious mould, so painfully visible in other churches we might mention; but everything we see, from the floor to the ceiling, from the altar to the organ, is both correct in taste, scrupulously clean, and in most beautiful, Church-like order. The Church consists of a nave, with a clerestory of twelve lights, and a handsome panelled roof adorned with Christian monograms and devices,—two side aisles,—two chancel chapels, named respectively *Troutbeck's* and *St. Catherine's*,—and a spacious chancel, in which are some elaborately carved stalls and open seats. So rapidly as stolid prejudice will admit, this uniform style of seat will be adopted throughout the Church.

The monuments within the Church are of considerable interest. One there is, in the north aisle, profuse in heraldic display, to the imperishable memory of the four RANDAL HOLMES, local antiquaries and heralds of considerable note, whose united Cheshire collections fill more than 250 MS. volumes in the British Museum. The third Randal was the author of that extraordinary and scarce heraldic work,—the "Academy of Armory" published in 1688. An elegant modern brass, and two altar-tombs of curious workmanship, adorn St. Catherine's Chapel, at the end of this aisle. One of the latter remembers Thomas Gamull, Recorder of Chester in 1613, son of Edmund Gamull, aforetime Mayor of Chester, and father of the celebrated royalist Sir Francis Gamull, who suffered sequestration of his estates during the Usurpation. The recumbent figures of the Recorder and his wife Alice appear upon the tomb; and at the feet of the lady kneels their infant son, afterwards the loyal Sir Francis Gamull. Their three infant daughters, holding skulls in their hands, and two elaborate shields of arms, ornament the side of the tomb. A similar tomb near bears the half-recumbent effigy of Philip Oldfield of Bradwall, dressed in the costume of the period, with a long gown and ruff, and a roll in his left hand. The figures of his four sons, each bearing a shield of arms, support the slab on which he leans, and between them a painted skeleton, in a similar attitude to the effigy, appears on the side of the tomb. Two daughters kneel at his head, and these also bear shields, in token of their marriage. Both these monuments are deserving the attention of the curious.

One of the north windows, by the side of these relics, is filled with stained glass. The east window also of this aisle, attracting the eye of the visitor the moment he enters, has just been adorned with an obituary memorial of intense national interest. Erected by public subscription, this window commemorates the glorious deeds of the gallant 23rd Regiment (Royal Welsh Fusileers) at the battles of Alma, Inkermann, and Sebastopol in 1854–5. The 23rd is a regiment highly esteemed by the Cestrians, nay, almost regarded by them as their own; and most of those brave spirits, officers and men, who nobly fell "with their faces to the foe" on those hard-won fields, had but a few months before regularly attended divine service at ST. MARY'S CHURCH. The subject represented in the window is Aaron and Hur holding up the hands of Moses, while the patriarch blesses the warring hosts of Israel; for as we read, in Exodus xvii. ver. 11, 12, "Moses' hands were heavy, and Aaron and Hur stayed up his hands, the one on the one side, and the other on the other; for it came to pass, that when Moses held up his hands Israel prevailed, and when his hands fell down, Amalek prevailed." It is a pretty and appropriate subject for such a memorial as this, implying the Christian Soldier's dependence upon the God of Battles!

The chancel, and Troutbeck chapel in the south aisle, also contain some tasteful and appropriate painted windows, ancient and modern; and on the south wall of the latter were discovered, a few years ago, some curious remains of ancient mural painting, representing the *Crucifixion* and *Resurrection* in curious juxtaposition with the figures of a *King*, a *Bishop*, and the *red and white roses* of York and Lancaster. The many beautiful monuments once embellishing the Troutbeck aisle were destroyed by the falling in of the roof in 1660. In bidding adieu to the church of *St. Mary the Virgin*, we may confidently assert that *"ne vile fano"* is the motto of Mr. Massie, the present rector, [77] for a neater and better ordered church we have not yet met with in our tour through the city.

Once more returning to Lower Bridge Street, we have before us the BRIDGEGATE, and two or three choice but eccentric-looking houses of the wood and plaster type, as depicted in our engraving.

Passing under the BRIDGEGATE, by the DEE MILLS and OLD BRIDGE, we might, if we chose, wander forth into HANDBRIDGE, were there anything in that suburb deserving our especial notice. As it is, however, we will make good our return to THE CROSS, and pursue, in the next chapter, our peregrinations through the Streets of "rare old Chester!"

The Bridge Gate.

The view here engraved affords a capital idea of the old timber houses still glorifying the city; while we gain, at the same time, such a prospect of the BRIDGE GATE as is not to be obtained from any other point.

CHAPTER VIII.

Northgate Street.—Commercial Buildings.—The Rows.—The Exchange.—Music Hall and Old Theatre.—Chester Cathedral.—St. Oswald's Church.—The Cloisters and Chapter-House.—Promptuarium, Refectory, and King's School.

OUR tours of inspection have, so far, been all down hill; let us now, then, take higher ground, and move glibly onward up NORTHGATE STREET.

Passing ST. PETER'S CHURCH, at the corner of the street, we come immediately to that classic pile of white freestone—the COMMERCIAL BUILDINGS AND NEWS ROOM, erected in 1808, from the designs of Mr. T. Harrison, the architect of the CASTLE and of the GROSVENOR BRIDGE.

To this succeeds SHOEMAKER'S ROW, extending about a hundred yards along the left side of the street. The Row upon the right hand used formerly to be known as *Broken-shin Row*, from the rugged and uneven character of the thoroughfare, and the manifest dangers that threatened the *shins* of those who ventured along it. Originally it is said to have been double its present length; but modern innovation—that wolf in sheep's clothing—has here, as elsewhere, played terrible havoc with "ye good olde citie."

A little higher up than this latter-named Row, we may profitably turn round, and survey, from this slight eminence, the lower part of the Street we have just traversed, together with the curious architecture of the houses in *Shoemaker's Row*. The scene is a picturesque one, with its oddly-carved beams and overhanging gables, which look as if ready to fall down on the beholder. But in order more fully to impress it on your memory, we present you farther on with a faithful sketch of NORTHGATE STREET, as seen from this point.

Onward we go, until an open space upon our left introduces us to the Market-Place of Chester's famed city. The market for vegetables is held in this area, with no other covering save the "bright blue sky;" but the sale of fish is conducted in that airy looking building, which occupies, we will not say *adorns*, the lower end of the Market-Place.

Northgate Street.

But what is yon new-looking structure, overlooking the Marketplace? *New*, did you say? Why, it is not very far from a couple of hundred years since that building, the EXCHANGE, first delighted the eyes of the old-fashioned citizens. True, the stone-work has been lately restored, and the bricks newly pointed; but practically this is the same EXCHANGE which, in 1698, was completed at a cost of 1000*l*.,—Roger Whitley, the then Mayor, being a large contributor. The statue embellishing yonder niche on the south front is a graceful representation of Queen Anne, of glorious memory, in her coronation robes,—a work which must have emanated from no mean chisel. The superstructure of the EXCHANGE stood originally upon four rows of stone columns, the ground floor being otherwise entirely open; but in 1756, just a hundred years ago, owing to some well-grounded fears for the safety of the structure, the lower tiers of shops, &c., were erected, as an extra support to the fabric; the greater portion of these are now occupied as police-offices, lock-ups, &c. On the higher story are the *Assembly Room*, the *Pentice* or *Council Chamber*, and the spacious *Town Hall*. The *Assembly Room* was a popular resort in the last generation, when corporation feasts, redolent of venison and primest turtle, were perpetually being discussed there; but it is many a long day since these savoury viands graced the aldermanic board. Oh, for the good old days! The winter Assemblies, too, wont to be held here, are now transferred to more congenial quarters at the Royal Hotel. The *Town Hall*, which is the *Common Hall* of the city, is a noble apartment, the walls ornamented with full-length portraits of numerous city notables, among whom figure Recorders Townsend, Leycester, Comberbach, and Williams; and Sirs Henry Bunbury, and John

Egerton, members for the city, of eminence in their day. Here are held the Quarter Sessions for the city, official public meetings, and the Elections for the city representatives in parliament. Immediately beyond this room is the *Pentice* or Council Chamber, where the mayor and magistrates settle the accounts of the drunk and disorderly, and take preliminary depositions in cases of felony, &c. This room, in which the Mayor is also annually chosen by the Council, has on its walls full-length portraits of George III., several members of the Grosvenor family, and of William Cross, Esq., the first Reform Mayor of Chester. Yonder series of large panels, contain portraits of Owen Jones, Offley, and other famous benefactors to the poor of the city. In a room in Abbey Square, the *City Records*, extending from the reign of the first Edward to the present time, are wretchedly huddled together— we wish we could say *preserved*; but surely the day is not far distant when a custodian of these important documents shall be appointed by the Council,—one who shall not only understand, but also *glorify* his office; then will many a dark epoch in the city's history be unravelled, and many a fact revealed which now lies hidden in the dust of obscurity.

Exchange, and Markets.

Opposite to the EXCHANGE is SAINT WERBURGH STREET, down which we must straightway roam, having a glorious treat awaiting us, in our long-promised visit to CHESTER CATHEDRAL.

But before we set foot within the sacred fane, let us proceed a little further, in order to examine yonder stately-looking pile, only just completed,—to wit, the NEW MUSIC HALL. Perhaps no structure within the city has undergone greater or more numerous changes of character than the shell of the one we are now surveying. The first we hear of it is as the Chapel of St. Nicholas, built, it is supposed, early in the fourteenth century. About this time, we read that the monks of St. Werburgh (monks were greedy dogs!), wishing to have the whole Cathedral to themselves, transferred the parish Church of St. Oswald, then as now occupying the south transept of the Cathedral, to this Chapel of St. Nicholas, which latter had perhaps been built with that idea "looming in the future." But the parishioners and corporation repudiated the change, and after much litigation recovered their old parish Church,—so the chapel of St. Nicholas was speedily deserted. After being "to let" for some fifty or sixty years, we next hear of it as the COMMON HALL of the city, removed here from Common-hall Street in 1545. In this service it remained, the arena of *law*, if not of *justice* (for the two do not always go hand in hand), until 1698, when the magisterial chair was removed to its present resting-place in the EXCHANGE. The third phase in its existence was its conversion into the warehouse of a common carrier, and into a mart for the sale of *wool*; the name it then bore was the WOOL HALL. Again was St. Nicholas the victim of transformation; for, at least as early as the year 1727, the walls, which once echoed forth the sounds of prayer and praise, were made to ring with the ribald jests of a common *playhouse*. Thirty years afterwards, there were two Theatres open at one time in Chester,—one *here*, and the other at the Tennis Court in Foregate Street; but about 1768, the latter establishment was closed up, and its "galaxy of talent" transferred to the Wool Hall. In 1777, the necessary patent from the crown was obtained for the licensing of the premises, and the Wool Hall forthwith developed into a THEATRE ROYAL. We will not stay to run over the numerous "stars" which have from time to time graced this theatrical firmament; it is enough to know that this "light of other days has faded" away, and that, so far as this building is concerned, the Chester Theatre exists only as matter of history.

In 1854-5, the Theatre was wholly obliterated, and the building in great part taken down; but the massive buttresses and sidelight arches of the original ecclesiastical structure were suffered to remain, and are yet plainly visible upon the north and south sides of the building. And now comes the last scene of the drama,—the scene we are now contemplating. On the ruins of the fallen Theatre, and on the foundation walls of the ancient Chapel of St. Nicholas, modern enterprise has raised a pile more in unison with its first estate, and far more worthy its close proximity to the Cathedral,—the NEW MUSIC HALL. The Hall has been erected from the designs of Mr. James Harrison, architect, whose other important works about the city we have already noticed. Its peculiar position, beset with heavy private buildings on three of its sides, prevented much attention being paid to the exterior; but the east front, being comparatively free, has afforded Mr. Harrison an opportunity for displaying his professional skill. Seen from the other end of St. Werburgh's Place, the handsome Tudor windows and porch of this front have a rich and truly picturesque effect; our artist, however, has chosen a nearer view, in order to give strength and definition to his sketch. In addition to a refreshment room, ladies' waiting and retiring rooms, and other offices, the interior presents to us a large and noble hall, 108 feet long, 40 feet wide, and 50 feet high, capable, with its two handsome galleries, of accommodating an audience of 1400 people. Its spacious orchestra, adorned with an organ of superior excellence, by Jackson, has ample room for 250 performers. The neatly panelled roof, resting upon shafted cross-beams tastefully ornamented, gives to the CHESTER MUSIC HALL a richness and elegance wholly unapproached by any similar room in the city. The Hall is, in every respect, a credit alike to the architect and to the city; and it is not too much to add that Mr. J. D. Williams, the builder and decorator of the structure, has done his part of the work faithfully and well. One man only was killed during the progress of the works, by an accidental fall from the ceiling of the Hall. It was opened Nov. 26, 1855, with a grand concert, at which Clara Novello and others officiated.

Music Hall, and Consistory Court.

And now for our long-deferred visit to the venerable CATHEDRAL. Turning aside from the Music Hall, we pass a small gate, and are at once in close communion with the south-west side of this massive structure. We can see from this point, distinctly enough, the ancient cruciform character of the edifice, that fittest symbolical form of a Christian Church; the east end forming the choir and Lady Chapel,—the south transept the Parish Church of St. Oswald,—the north transept almost unappropriated,—and the west end the nave, into which latter we are now passing through a rich and handsome Tudor porch. And here let us observe that, as our knowledge of architectural detail is unhappily small, we must rely for our descriptions on the "dogmatic teaching" of other and abler heads. But first a word or two on the foundation and history of this fine old CATHEDRAL.

Tradition avers that under the imperial dominion of pagan Rome, a temple, dedicated to Apollo, occupied the spot now consecrated to the Triune God; and that this temple had itself supplanted a still older fane of the superstitious Druids. However this may be, it is an historical fact, amply corroborated, that Wulpherus, King of the Mercians, who flourished about A.D. 660, and Ermenilde, his queen, perceiving the attachment of their daughter, St. Werburgh, to a religious life, built an Abbey at Chester, for her and such other pious ladies who should, in like manner, prefer a conventual life. To St. Peter and St. Paul this Saxon Abbey was dedicated. St. Werburgh, being prioress or patron of three Abbeys—Chester, Trentham, and Hanbury—died and was buried in the latter edifice; but owing to the threatened incursions of the Danes, her sacred relics were thence removed, two hundred years afterwards, to Chester, for greater security, and lodged in the Abbey her royal father had founded in her honour. About 907, Ethelfleda, Countess of Mercia, erected on the same site a nobler Abbey, dedicated to her whose shrine then rested there—the immaculate St. Werburgh. Thus matters remained for nearly two centuries, when Earl Hugh Lupus, nephew and favourite of the Conqueror, having lived a life of debauchery and excess, compounded for his sins by the erection of an edifice larger and more splendid than the last, founding there a Monastery of St. Bennet's order, under the superintendence of Anselm, then abbot of Bec, in Normandy, afterwards Archbishop of Canterbury. A day or two before his death, Earl Hugh was shorn a monk of the Abbey his own remorseful bounty had founded. Immense possessions accrued to the Abbey, both from Hugh Lupus, the founder, and from his successors in the earldom. Early in the reign of Edward I., and in the abbacy of Simon *de Albo Monasterio* (Whitchurch), the rebuilding of the Abbey was commenced. It continued slowly to progress, under succeeding abbots, for about two hundred years, and until Abbot *Simon Ripley* virtually completed, in 1492, the erection of the Cathedral as we see it in the present day. Only fifty years afterwards, the foul blast of destruction fell like an avalanche upon the monastic institutions of Britain—Chester among the number. Bluff King Hal, that shameless polygamist, in a fit of pretended religious zeal, dissolved all these fraternities, and, pocketing the spoil, dealt out their lands to his creatures with right royal munificence. True, he left us the *shell*, in his new foundation of a Cathedral and Chapter; but he gulped up the *kernel* in the shape of the manorial possessions of the Abbey. John Bird was the first peculiar Bishop of Chester; and Thomas Clarke transposed himself from the last Romanist Abbot to the first Protestant Dean of Chester.

Entering the CATHEDRAL by the South Porch, we find ourselves in the NAVE, and close to a lofty chamber now used as the Consistory Court. Here are tried, before the chancellor of the diocese, the validity or otherwise of disputed wills, actions for slander, and other causes falling within the province of ecclesiastical law. Beyond, and to the left of this Court, near the baptismal font, is the great West Entrance of the Cathedral, built during the energetic rule of the Abbot Simon Ripley. It was the design of Ripley to erect two massive towers at this end of the Cathedral, and the foundations of these towers are still existing there; but owing to an unexpected "fall in the funds," or to some other cause, the original intention was never carried out.

The West Entrance, as we now behold it, has a large and magnificent window of delicate tracery, recently filled with a series of designs in stained glass, illustrating the final sentence of the Apostles' Creed, "The Resurrection of the Body, and the Life Everlasting." In the centre of the main opening, we have the "Appearance of our Lord to St. Mary Magdalene in the Garden;" and beneath, "Our Lord's Supper with the Disciples at Emmaus." The three lights south of the centre illustrate the "Resurrection of our Lord," above Whom are seen the Heavenly Host, while below are the affrighted soldiers, the angel at the tomb, with the apostles and holy women. In the three divisions on the north side is depicted "Our Lord in Judgment," surrounded by the patriarchs, prophets, apostles, and saints: beneath is the Archangel Michael trampling upon Satan, with groups of "the Just" on their way up to Heaven, accompanied by guardian angels. The rich tracery overhead is filled with the "Genealogical Tree of our Lord," commencing with the reclining figure of Jesse, and its branches spreading through more than one hundred openings, finishing with the birth, death, and glorification of Jesus Christ. This is a memorial window, erected by the widow of the Rev. P. W. Hamilton, of Hoole, near Chester, and cannot fail to be an object of surpassing interest to every visitor. It was designed and executed by Messrs. M. and A. O'Connor, of London.

West Entrance of the Cathedral.

The door being open, let us step out to the open air, and refresh our eyes with a momentary glance at the WEST ENTRANCE OF THE CATHEDRAL. This is, externally, the most beautiful remaining portion of this glorious edifice. Time has, of course, been at work here, as elsewhere, gnawing away at the old red sandstone; but there is still enough left to give us an idea of its ancient beauty.

> Forms of saints are meekly kneeling
> The Cathedral door above:

the which door is a beautiful double Tudor arch of chaste design, supported on either side by four canopied niches, once ornamented with statuettes, but now fast going to decay. Over this is the great west window of eight lights, the whole flanked by two fine octagonal turrets with embattled parapets. Altogether, this front is a sight grateful to look upon, but one eminently suggestive of the ephemeral character of all things here below.

Returning to the Nave, we find at the head of the north aisle a flight of stairs leading up through the arched doorway into the Episcopal Palace; through this door the bishop ordinarily enters the Cathedral in his robes. The external wall of this aisle is one of the most ancient portions of the entire structure, being part of the Norman edifice of Hugh Lupus. It has two doors, one at each end, opening to the east and west walks of the CLOISTERS, of which more anon. The windows of the Nave and of the clerestory above it, are all of the perpendicular character, and throw a flood of dim religious light into the interior. There is but one stained-glass window, and *that* an obituary one, in the south aisle of the nave. Numerous monuments deck the walls, and disfigure the pillars of the nave, conspicuous among which are those to Dean Smith, translator of Longinus, Thucydides, and other classic authors; also memorials of the Mainwaring, Dod, Buchanan, Matthews, Ward, and Hilton families. One in the north aisle to the memory of Captain John Moore Napier, who died in India of Asiatic cholera, is worthy of special remark, from the spirited and touching epitaph, written by his uncle, that brave and gallant soldier, Sir Charles Napier, the veteran hero of Scinde. It runs thus:—

> The tomb is no record of high lineage;
> His may be traced by his name.
> His race was one of soldiers;
> Among soldiers he lived, among them he died,
> A soldier falling where numbers fell with him
> In a barbarous land.
> Yet there died none more generous,
> More daring, more gifted, more religious.
> On his early grave
> Fell the tears of stern and hardy men,
> As his had fallen on the grave of others.

True poetry this, albeit expressed in modest prose! The Nave is 160 feet long, 74½ feet wide, and 78 feet high.

The following are the present dignitaries of the Cathedral:—

BISHOP—The Right Rev. John Graham, D.D.
DEAN—The Very Reverend Frederick Anson, D.D.

ARCHDEACONS.	
Ven. Isaac Wood, Middlewich.	Ven. John Jones, Liverpool.
CANONS.	
Rev. James Slade, M.A.	Rev. Thomas Eaton, M.A.
Rev. George B. Blomfield, M.A.	Rev. Temple Hillyard, M.A.
HONORARY CANONS.	
Rev. C. A. Thurlow, M.A.	Rev. Hugh Stowell, M.A.
Rev. Hugh McNeile, D.D.	Rev. William Cooke, M.A.

MINOR CANONS.	
Rev. W. Harrison, M.A.	Rev. R. M. Smith, M.A.
Rev. E. F. Thurland, Precentor.	Rev. H. Venables, M.A.

Through an oaken door at the extremity of the north aisle, we pass into the north wing of the Transept,—like the Nave, not appropriated to any of the ordinary services of the church. The lower portion of its walls is indisputably Norman work, as is evidenced by the seven-arched triforium, which traverses midway its eastern side. A small doorway in the corner of this wall leads up, by a spiral staircase, to the triforium and great tower, as also to the clerestory gallery, which "threads its devious course" almost wholly round the sacred edifice. The archway under the great north window of the Transept conducts to the Chapter House and Cathedral Library. Two monuments in this wing deserve our notice,—one to the memory of Sir John Grey Egerton, Bart., sometime M.P. for Chester,—and the other to Colonel Roger Barnston, of Chester, erected by the subscriptions of his admiring friends and fellow-citizens. Immediately over the monument of Sir John Egerton is placed a piece of magnificent tapestry, copied from one of Raphael's masterpieces, representing "Elymas the sorcerer struck with blindness before Sergius Paulus." This is stated to have been brought over from a nunnery in France, and, until the recent alterations, usurped the place of the reredos at the back of the High Altar.

Thence returning to the Nave, we pass under the massive stone screen into the CHOIR, and are at once filled with admiration of its noble proportions, and of the taste and elegance which everywhere pervade it. The great features of the structure we have hitherto examined have been chiefly architectural, but here we are introduced to a scene in which all the resources of human art have been brought to bear by the creature man in honour of his Creator God. Look at this gorgeous canopy of ancient oak, adorning and supporting the fine organ overhead—at that magnificent range of Stalls, also of old oak, four-and-twenty on either side, crowned with canopies of the richest tracery, no one stall a copy of the other—at those pews of fairest form and choicest elaboration—at yon Shrine of St. Werburgh, now the Episcopal Throne—at the handsome stone pulpit—at the bold oak lectern, the eagle bearing upon his wings the glad tidings of salvation—at the graceful Altar-screen and Holy Table—and at the stained-glass enrichments of the two great east windows, through which gleams the morning sun,

Dyed
In the soft chequerings of a sleepy light.—

As all these meet our wondering eyes, then do we awake to the consciousness that this is the Lord's House, and, as it richly deserves to be, the Mother Church of the city and diocese. The seats of the STALLS, or *misericordiæ*, are worthy of our inspection, every one bearing some device different from its companions. The THRONE is composed, in great part, of the pedestal on which rested, in Romish days, the sacred relics of St. Werburgh,—those relics which, according to Father Bradshaw, performed such great and astounding miracles. The images surrounding it are supposed to be those of Mercian kings and saints, to which royal line St. Werburgh belonged. The Throne has been improved and raised some feet within the last fifteen years. The stone PULPIT replaced an older one of monarch oak, which has since been transformed into a long open seat for the Lady Chapel. The Communion Table and its appointments are all in good taste; and the elegant stone REREDOS, which divides the ALTAR from the Lady Chapel, is of exceedingly chaste and appropriate character. The subjects in the east clerestory window represent "Our blessed Lord between the four Evangelists," over whom are depicted five incidents in Christ's career on earth,—the Agony in the Garden—Jesus bearing His Cross—the Crucifixion—the Resurrection—and the Ascension. The entire length of the CHOIR is 125 feet, breadth 74½ feet, and height 78 feet.

The north aisle of the Choir has one stained-glass obituary window, but no other object of interest, save a few old monuments, and a vestry for the Canons, the latter being a portion of the old Norman edifice. We pass hence to the LADY CHAPEL, at the east end of the Choir, supposed by some to be the oldest portion of the present re-edified Cathedral. It is 65 feet long, 74½ feet wide, including the side aisles, and 33 feet high. The Chapel consisted originally of one central aisle only, the two side aisles having been added at a later period. At the east end stood the Shrine of St. Werburgh, until the Reformation saw it removed to the Choir, and converted thenceforward into the Bishop's Throne. The east window of the Lady Chapel is embellished with stained glass of the richest description—the subjects being severally, the Annunciation, the Nativity, the Wise Men's Offering, the Presentation in the Temple, Christ disputing with the Doctors, the Baptism of John, the Water turned into Wine, Healing the Lame, Walking on the Sea, Feeding the Multitude, the Transfiguration, the Raising of Lazarus, the Entry into Jerusalem, Washing the Disciples' Feet, and the Last Supper,—the whole crowned with symbolical figures of the Twelve Apostles. In this Chapel George Marsh was condemned to be burnt for heresy in the days of Queen Mary.

The south aisle of the Choir and Lady Chapel has all its windows adorned with stained glass, the one at the east end being an obituary memorial for the late Hugh Robert Hughes, Esq., of the Bache, erected by his son, inheritor from his uncle, Lord Dinorben, of Kinmel Park, Flintshire. Obituary windows to the Humberston and Anson families, and two others piously erected by the present worthy Dean, complete the adornment of this aisle. Dean Anson has done more to beautify his Cathedral than all his predecessors put together! Under an indented arch in the east wall recline the dust and ashes of one of the abbots of St. Werburgh, the slab adorned with a cross *floree*. In the centre of this aisle stands an altar-tomb, once built into the wall of the Sedilia. This tomb tradition assigns to Henry IV. of Germany; but it appears that monarch died and was buried in his own dominions: other and better authority surmises it to be the tomb of one of the later abbots.

From this aisle we pass into the south wing of the Transept, time out of mind appropriated to the parish CHURCH OF ST. OSWALD. So early as the ninth century, a Church existed here, independent of the Abbey; but on the enlargement of the latter in the thirteenth century, St. Oswald's became incorporated with the Abbey, as its southern transept. This was the Church, the functions of which were transferred by the monks to St. Nicholas Chapel, now the MUSIC HALL; but the parishioners could not forget their first love, and soon wormed their way back again to St. Oswald's. The Church contains some handsome monuments, worthy the attention of the visitor.

Crossing the nave, we see opposite to us a door, introducing us to the CLOISTERS of this once powerful Abbey. The arch we are now passing under is a Norman specimen of exceeding purity; and disfigured as it has been by modern *improvements*, yet affords a high degree of interest to the intelligent antiquary. The CLOISTERS once formed a quadrangle of 110 feet square; but the south portion has almost entirely disappeared, the bases of some of the pillars alone remaining. The east walk has a doorway leading into the CHAPTER HOUSE, through a vaulted Vestibule of great architectural beauty. These two apartments were the favourite places of sepulture of the puissant Norman earls, as well as of the earlier abbots of the Monastery. In the Chapter House, which is a noble building of the twelfth century, are deposited the Cathedral Library, as well as some vestiges of antiquity found within the Abbey and its precincts. Of these, a part of the stone coffin of Abbot Simon Ripley, and a Roman red sandstone inscription found near the present Deanery, are the most prominent and interesting. Over the door hang two bullet-tattered flags, once belonging to the 22nd (Cheshire) Regiment. A passage beyond the Chapter House leads, by the Maiden's Walk, into the Abbey Court; and a doorway at the northwest corner to the Dormitory, now totally destroyed. A beautiful Norman chamber runs along the side of the western walk, and is variously designated the Promptuarium and *Abbot's Hall*. This apartment, although an engraving of it appeared in Ormerod's "History of Cheshire," was but little known to Chester antiquaries until the year 1849, when this city was honoured with a visit from the British Archæological Association. A vast amount of rubbish, the accumulation of centuries, at that period blocked up the chamber; but the greater part of it was removed at the expense of the Association, and an able paper delivered on the subject, by Mr. Ashpitel, at their Chester Congress. That gentleman pronounced it to be the *Promptuarium*, or *Buttery* of the Abbey; but a room, originally 105 feet long, seems of undue proportions for such a purpose. Mr. W. F. Ayrton, Secretary of the Chester Archæological Society, with greater apparent probability conceives it to be the *secunda aula* of the Monastery, such as we find described in the charter of Henry VIII. Here it was that audience was given to strangers and dependants, and where friends of the abbot were temporarily entertained during their visits to the Monastery.

The wall of the obliterated south walk, notwithstanding the cloister itself is 'no more,' is yet not without interest to the real lover of antiquity. Two rude arcades of late Norman work stretch along this wall, the arches of which mark the place of sepulture of four early abbots of the foundation. Some of the bases of the pillars once supporting the roof of the south walk are still visible on the Preese, or Cloister Green.

Returning to the north walk, we pass thence, under a richly ornamented arch, into another apartment on the right hand, now and for three centuries past occupied as the GRAMMAR SCHOOL of the Cathedral. Few portions of the conventual buildings are so little known to visitors as the one we are now entering,—few will so amply repay their inspection as will this, the ancient REFECTORY of this once famous Monastery. Time was,

> And a gay time it was then, O!

when this noble apartment, the *Frater House* of the Abbey, re-echoed with the sounds of feast and revelry,—when the monks of St. Werburgh, and their privileged friends, discussed, in joyous mood, the good things of this life, dished up to them from the kitchens and buttery of the Abbey. Fancy how the tables groaned with the savoury venison and other titbits from the granges of the abbot,—with the products of their favourite kaleyards and fisheries,—and their wines and liquors brought from beyond sea,—and say, if you think these degenerate times can show aught to equal those palmy days! After all, though

> Many have told of the monks of old,
>   What a saintly race they were;
> Yet 'tis most true that a merrier crew
>   Could scarce be found elsewhere.
>   For they sang and laughed,

>   And the rich wine quaffed,
>   And lived on the daintiest fare.
>
>   And the Abbot meek, with his form so sleek,
>   Was the heartiest of them all,
>   And would take his place, with a smiling face,
>   When the REFECTORY bell would call;
>   And they sang and laughed,
>   And the rich wine quaffed,
>   Till they shook the olden hall!

Say what you will of the austerities supposed to belong to the monastic life, those recluses of old lived a life as jolly, as careless, and as free, as the gayest of us in this 19th century! Yonder, at the head of that staircased recess in the south wall, is the ancient Oratory, from which one of the 'knights of the cowl' daily 'said grace,' and pronounced a classic oration, while his brethren were at meals in the spacious hall beneath him. Oh, what a sight for carnal eyes like his to dwell and gloat upon! But we must not soliloquise. The Fratry, or Refectory, in the days we are describing, was of nobler dimensions even than now; for it then extended some twenty or thirty feet farther westward, and was doubtless shorn of its fair proportions at the time the present road was constructed from the Abbey Square. This room, which is 98 feet long and 34 feet high, has a range of six pointed windows on the one side, and four on the other, and had once an eastern lancet-shaped window of considerable beauty. Of the window of the present day we forbear to speak; simply let us hope that the hour is at hand, when so hideous an abortion of all that is "chaste and beautiful in art" shall vanish from the scene, and be replaced by a window worthy of the apartment it was meant to adorn! The steps leading up to the Oratory communicated originally with the DORMITORY of the Abbey, which prior to the present century occupied the higher range of the eastern cloister, but has now entirely disappeared.

At the Reformation, when King Henry VIII. transformed the Abbey into a Cathedral, he founded here, in the thirty-sixth year of his reign, a GRAMMAR SCHOOL for twenty-four boys, and endowed it with a Head Master, and numerous privileges, some of which it was *our* lot, twenty years ago, personally to share. The history of the School, and of the many Cheshire worthies educated within its walls, would furnish matter for a distinct treatise, and it is not improbable that such may one day appear from our humble pen. For the present, then, we will retire from this scene of our boyhood's delight, and ascending the range of steps near the entrance door, emerge from the "bosom of our spiritual mother" at a point very close to the head of Abbey Street.

CHAPTER IX.

Abbey Square, Deanery, and Palace.—The Abbey Gates.—Chester Markets, and Abbot's Fair.—Northgate, and old City Gaol.—St. John's Hospital and Blue School.—Newtown, and Christ Church.—Railway Tunnel.—St. Thomas' Chapel.—Training College.

THE smell of sanctity yet fresh upon us, let us now continue, as best we may, our peregrinations northward.

Yonder, at the lower end of this Street, we catch a glimpse of the WALLS; and, turning ourselves about, take a rapid look at ABBEY SQUARE (the only Square old Chester can boast!) with its DEANERY and BISHOP'S PALACE,—the former occupying the site of the ancient CHAPEL OF ST. THOMAS, nay, resting indeed on the foundations of that sacred edifice. The latter is a gloomy-looking pile of red sandstone, erected by Bishop Keene in 1753; but within it have resided as goodly a fellowship of mitred heads as ever graced the episcopal bench. Markham, Porteus, Cleaver, Law, Blomfield, Sumner, and last not least, Graham, our present amiable diocesan, have each in turn found here their house and home.

But what is this massive and substantial structure, under which we are now passing,—so massive and strong as almost to have defied the ravages of time? Behold in it the principal GATEWAY of the ABBEY, an imposing edifice even in this our day, but one which had seen the meridian of its splendour ere Harry the Eighth, hypocritical Harry! sacrilegiously sealed and decreed its doom. In those, its halcyon days, few gates indeed might "stand between the wind and its nobility;" for 'regal pomp and lordly retinue' sought ever and anon a welcome here. And not in vain: for as we have already shown, when once its ponderous doors moved back to give them ingress, the tables of the Refectory and the *bonhommie* of the monks never failed to sustain the hospitable character of the Abbey. Look up, through the gloom, at the solid masonry of this ancient pile, and at the admirable groining which supports the superstructure;—gingerbread architecture was all unknown in those mediæval times! On the west side of the archway, we can still see the rust-coated staples, on which, three or four centuries ago, swang the oaken gates of the Abbey. Times have changed; and the hoary old porter, with his shaven scalp, and keys of 'trewyst steele,' has flitted away from the scene, while the tide of life now flows freely, and without obstruction, 'neath this venerable Gate. Here, in 1554, it is traditionally said that GEORGE MARSH, a 'champion for the glorious truth,' was first imprisoned, preparatory to his trial and martyrdom at the stake. And why,—what evil had he done? What was "the height and might of his offending?" Simply this,—that "after the manner that man then called heresy, so worshipped he the God of his fathers." The *heretics* of one age are not unfrequently the *saints* of another; and certain it is that the memory of Marsh and the faith he died for, gained rather than lost by those Marian fires! Not long afterwards, if not indeed before, this structure was turned into the Episcopal REGISTRY; and here are deposited, in its well-kept archives, the 'last wills and testaments' of all who have died, and 'left aught to leave,' within the scattered limits of this widespread diocese. The beautiful condition and systematic arrangement of these important records put other and similar Offices terribly to the blush, and are in the highest degree creditable to the zeal and ability of the present Registrar, Henry Raikes, Esq. [96] Half a century or so ago, the then deputy registrar was one Mr. Speed, a Joseph Andrews in his way, though scarcely perhaps so free from guile as that immaculate hero. Now it so happened that a frail daughter of Eve had found her way into Master Speed's domain, probably to administer to some *will* in his possession, or for divers other "urgent private affairs." While thus engaged, a party from without required Mr. Deputy's assistance; so locking the lady in the inner office, he turned to attend to his unseasonable visitor. Mademoiselle, finding herself immured, in so "wilful" a manner, in this dusky prison, and having the remembrance of MARSH and his martyrdom in her mind, became seriously alarmed. Having however, like most women, a "*will* of her own," she threw open the window which looks into Abbey Square, and springing out of it like a zephyr, quietly allowed herself to descend, buoyed up by her flowing garments, to the ground below! Some waggish artist has perpetuated the event in a characteristic sketch, displaying the "flight of the descending angel;" to which another sarcastic genius, the late Mascie Taylor, Esq., added this couplet:—

> Since women are so fond of men,
> With *Speed* she will fly up again!

Let us now pass on.

Leaving behind us the ABBEY GATE and its bygone associations, we are once more in NORTHGATE STREET, and may stay to cast "one withering glance" at those melancholy-looking buildings on either side, the FOWL, BUTTER, and BUTCHERS' MARKETS of the city. Hideous as specimens of architectural taste, destitute of convenience or comfort in use, furthermore heavy and cheerless to look upon, these Markets have, of themselves, nothing to rivet the attention of the sightseer. But the ground they stand on was in old time an open area; and here, from the time of the great Hugh Lupus to the glorious advent of the Reformation, did the monks of St. Werburgh hold their annual FAIR at the great feast of that saint. It was during one of these fairs that Earl Randle was besieged in Rhuddlan Castle by the Welsh, when attempting the subjugation of those Cambrian mountaineers. The Earl, perceiving the nice pickle he was in, despatched a messenger to De Lacy, his constable at Chester, a "ryght valiaunt manne," who, rushing into the Fair, presently collected to his standard a "noble army of fiddlers" and drunken musicians— the "tag, rag, and bobtail" there assembled—and with these he forthwith set out to the relief of his beleagured lord. The Welsh, who had previously felt sure of their prey, seeing the immense host approach, and hearing withal the terrible discords of "harp, flute, sackbut, psaltery, and other kinds of music," reasonably enough concluded that Bedlam was let loose; and with that doubtful sort of valour sometimes nicknamed discretion, precipitately took to their heels, and so raised the siege. The Earl returned to Chester at the head of his victorious minstrels, and immediately chartered the holding of this Fair with numerous privileges and immunities, granting to the brave De Lacy, and to his heirs for ever, the licensing of and custody over the "Minstrels of Cheshire;" which prerogative was regularly exercised by his descendants, until the middle of the last century. So much for the ABBOT'S FAIR, and the bloodless "fight of the fiddlers;"—we may now "fair"-ly enough continue our course of inspection.

Proceeding direct north, we come to another postern, now ruinated, the mere arch itself alone remaining. This is the *Little* or *Higher Abbey Gate*; and from it, in days past, ran the wall of the Monastery in a direct line southward to the Great ABBEY GATE; the wall itself has now given way to a row of shops and other valuable buildings.

Nearly opposite to the *Little Abbey Gate*, retiring somewhat from the street, stands a neat, modern-built house; in the courtyard of which we may see a handsome piece of statuary, purchased by a former proprietor at the close of the French War: it represents the British Lion,

> With tail erect and aspect terrible,

trampling majestically on the Eagle of France,—typical of the overthrow of the first Napoleon. Little did the sculptor suppose, when he proudly chiselled 'that angry mane, and tail of grim defiance,' that the Lion and the Eagle would so soon be united in such friendly bonds, nay even fighting, side by side, the almost unaided battle of right against might, justice against oppression! If that classic group had to be sculptured anew—

> Such are the strange mutations of the world,—

the prostrate Eagle might haply bear an additional head, emblematical of the ruthless despoiler of Finland, the Caucasus, and Poland!

In a step or two we are passing the higher end of *King Street*, formerly *Barn Lane*, at the corner of which stands an ancient hostelry, yclept the "Pied

Bull." Here again we have before us the degenerate type of those strange old Rows, which so filled you with amaze in our earlier rambles. There can be no doubt that, originally, these wondrous piazzas ran continuously along the four great streets of the city, except where they verge upon the confines of the Abbey; but these isolated portions are gradually disappearing before the "march of improvement." Doctors differ, alas! in Chester, as elsewhere, about the actual wisdom of this aforesaid "march!"

Again we move onwards, passing under a substantial arch of white stone, referred to in our "Walk round the Walls" as the NORTHGATE of the city. While the other three Gates were vested, by serjeantship, from time immemorial, in various noble families, this, the *porta septentrionalis*, as anciently belonged to the commorant citizens. Prior to 1808, when the present arch was erected, the NORTHGATE, if we may credit the engravings handed down to us, was a miserably effete and incongruous erection. What made it appear more so was the Gaol, or common prison of the city, which occupied a great part of the space around, above, and below it. A prison existed here from the earliest period; it is quoted in documents of the Norman earldom, and was at the time of its demolition a terrible specimen of legalised corruption—an establishment defying even the besom of a Howard to purge or purify. The city sheriff here saw execution done on all criminals capitally convicted within the county; here again the unfortunate debtor got "whitewashed," and relieved of his "little odd scores;" and here were practised those "tortures thrice refined" which might put even the Great Inquisition to the blush. Far away from human gaze, fathoms deep in the solid rock, were chambers hewn, dreadful to survey, horrifying to think upon. Of these, two bore the distinguishing titles of "Little Ease," and the "Dead Man's Room." The latter was the spot where condemned criminals awaited their execution, and was "a dark stinking place" in which snakes and other venomous reptiles gambolled at discretion. The "Little Ease," as we read from a contemporary work, "was a hole hewed out in a rock; the breadth and cross from side to side was seventeen inches from the back to the inside of the great door; at the top seven inches, at the shoulders eight inches, and at the breast nine inches and a-half; with *a device to lessen the height* as they were minded to torture the person put in, by drawboards which shot over across the two sides, to a yard in height, or thereabouts."

In those blissful times when Oliver Cromwell ruled England with an iron sceptre, these two "pleasantly situated furnished apartments" were in great request by the Barebones magistracy; and it is matter of record that,

> Locked in their cold embrace,

numerous unoffending, peaceloving Quakers endured the rod of persecution for conscience sake. And yet, forsooth, *those* were your oft-vaunted days of civil and religious liberty! Away with them all, say we! The Gaol, with its attendant miseries, has gone, but the dungeons we have pictured abide there still, beneath the ground we are now standing on,—though filled up, it is true, and for ever absolved from their ancient uses.

Having just passed *under* one arch, we are now walking *over* another which spans an abyss formed by the deep cut of the Ellesmere and Chester Canal. Yon little parallel archway, a few yards to the westward of us, is the *Bridge of Death*,—the path along which the felons about to die usually went to receive the "last consolation of the church" in the Chapel of St. John, on the opposite side of the gulf.

Northgate, and Bluecoat Hospital.

Pass we on once more for a few yards, and then turning round, a prospect awaits us the very similitude of that depicted in our engraving. To the left we have the NORTHGATE, and portion of the WALLS—those rare old Walls!—while the foreground to the right is occupied by that useful charitable institution, the BLUE-COAT HOSPITAL. For centuries prior to the great Civil War there stood, on this site, a venerable asylum, founded by Randal, Earl of Chester, for "poore and sillie persons," under the name of the HOSPITAL OF ST. JOHN THE BAPTIST. In the reign of Edward III., a jury of free citizens was sworn to report on the "vested rights" of this house, and the verdict these worthies returned was this:—

> "That there ought to be, and have accustomed to be, in the said Hospital, three chaplains to say mass daily—two in the church, and the third in the chapel—before the poor and feeble sustained in the said Hospital; and that one lamp ought to be sustained at mass every day in the

> said Hospital, and to burn every night in the whole year; and that thirteen beds, competently clothed, should be sustained in the same Hospital, and receive thirteen poor men of the same city; whereof each shall have for daily allowance a loaf of bread, a dish of pottage, half a gallon of competent ale, and a piece of fish or flesh, as the day shall require."

Not bad fare this for the thirteen brethren, "poore and feeble," who, from all we can judge,

> Must have gone to bed merry (as who could fail),
> On their foaming "half-gallons of competent ale!"

Thus matters sped with this thriving community for several hundred years; and even at the Reformation, when other and similar institutions foundered in the gale, St. John's Hospital appears to have weathered the storm. It might, indeed, have retained until now its original position, had not England got entangled in that horrid Civil War. Then it was that, with characteristic loyalty, the men of old Chester declared for the king—then it was that the suburbs of the city became a ruinous heap—and that this venerable Hospital was razed to the ground, lest it should serve as a cover for the artillery of the enemy. But the city, which had so bravely withstood one foe, had, like the Kars of our own day, to succumb before another; for famine at length achieved what the deadly cannon had failed to accomplish! The tale of the SIEGE has already been told; suffice it then to say, that order and the monarchy being once more restored, the site of the Hospital, and the lands belonging to it, were granted by Charles II. to Colonel Whitley, and at his death to the Mayor and Corporation of Chester, as permanent custodians of the charity. How the Corporation abused their trust, and mismanaged the Hospital; how they sold its estates, and squandered the proceeds; and how, after all, "like leeches satiate with evil blood," they had to disgorge their plunder, is, we can assure you, a very pretty story, which we might tell, if we chose, but we are mercifully inclined.

A BLUE-COAT HOSPITAL was established in Chester in 1700, under the auspices of Bishop Stratford; and, seventeen years afterwards, the liberality of the citizens erected in its service a "local habitation," on part of the site originally occupied by the Hospital of St. John. But bricks and mortar, like everything else, will not last for ever; so the old premises having gone to decay, benevolence has again put its shoulder to the wheel, and, in 1854, restored the fabric in the handsome manner we now behold it. That graceful little statue over the doorway—a portrait of one of the "Blue Boys"—is a study from the life by Richardson, of London. There are thirty-one scholars on the foundation, all clothed, fed, boarded, and educated at the cost of the charity; besides which, there is a probationary or "GREEN CAP" SCHOOL, from which those who have "attained the purple" are usually selected.

As for the "thirteen brethren, poore and feeble," of the original foundation, their number, which, from causes already hinted at, had dwindled down to six, has recently been restored,—their cottages at the rear of the Blue School rebuilt, and fitted with every convenience,—while each brother and sister now receives an allowance of ten shillings per week. Thus, thanks to Lord Brougham and his charity commissioners, thirteen poor souls—

> From chilling want and guilty murmurs free,

here rest their aged limbs; and as they, in turn, go down peacefully to the grave, others will step into their shoes, to the perpetual honour of the HOSPITAL OF ST. JOHN, and of its Norman founder, the good Earl Randal.

The steep lane running westward from the Hospital is CANAL STREET, leading down to the canal, and the "banks of the Dee." You don't care about going down there, just now? Very well, then, we'll refrain; but, uninviting as it seems at first sight, a ramble upon the Navigation Cop, at the first flow of the tide, is an enjoyable sort of treat, as you'll find if you have time to avail yourself of it.

Nearly opposite to the Blue School is GEORGE STREET, anciently called *Gorse Stacks*, a wider and more commodious street than the last, leading away to the Cattle Market and Railway Station, as also to the populous and increasing suburb of NEW TOWN. We can remember this locality when it was little else but green pasture—the *Lion's Field* we believe it was called—but how changed is it now! its verdure has fled,—it is country no longer; for the once open fields now swarm with innumerable homes of men! Near the bottom of ST. ANN STREET, the oldest and still principal street of this suburb, stands CHRIST CHURCH, a neat little cruciform structure, with diminutive spire, and small lancet-shaped windows, erected in 1838, to meet the spiritual wants of this growing neighbourhood. The Church has sitting accommodation for about 600 worshippers.

Proceeding along UPPER NORTHGATE STREET, we soon reach Egerton House, formerly a seat of the Cheshire family of that name; but recently converted into a first-class ladies' school, under the efficient management of the Misses Williams. Stay here an instant, for we are just over the TUNNEL of the Chester and Holyhead Railway, which science, art, and convenience have combined to make the great highway between England and Ireland.

A little farther on, and our street branches off in two almost parallel directions,—the way upon our right being the old coach road to Birkenhead and Liverpool, and that upon our left—but stay! we are travelling a "leetle" too fast, for we haven't quite done with our present *locale*. Before us stands a lofty house, crowned with a lanthorn-shaped observatory, and at present the residence of Mr. Fletcher. It occupies the site of an older house, called at different periods *Green Hall* and *Jolly's Hall*, destroyed before the Siege of Chester, for the same reasons which dictated the fall of other portions of the suburbs. This house, again, had usurped the place of an older tenant of the soil; for here was situate the CHAPEL and CEMETERY of ST. THOMAS À BECKET, founded, no doubt, soon after that prelate's murder and canonisation in 1170. This Chapel gave name to the manorial court in connection with the Abbey, to which jurisdiction the tenants of the Cathedral are even now subject. Until lately, the bailiff of the Dean and Chapter held his annual court for this manor in the Refectory (now the King's School), impanelling his jury from among the Cathedral tenants, who, by that "suit and service," acknowledged the prerogative of this ancient court. Now let us pass on along the roadway to our left.

What is this Elizabethan building we are so rapidly approaching? Surely this has no antediluvian tale to tell—no musty connection with mediæval times? No, truly: here we have a creation of the present age—a noble institution,—one which, from its character and objects, deserves at least some notice at our hands. This is the DIOCESAN TRAINING COLLEGE, the same building we saw and admired at a distance, in our "Walk round the Walls." Erected mainly by public subscription, in 1842, from the designs of Messrs. Buckler, of London—established for the training and qualifying of masters for the Church Schools of the diocese,—presided over by the bishop, and more immediately by the talented principal, the Rev. Arthur Rigg,—this institution "pursues the even tenour of its way," by annually preparing a number of young men fitted for the duties of parochial schoolmasters—men firmly attached to the Church of their forefathers, and able to impart to those intrusted to them the blessings of a sound, religious, and useful education.

The COLLEGE has a resident principal and vice-principal, the former, Mr. Rigg, having held his appointment since the first starting of the project. In its infancy, and while the present handsome edifice was in building, the COLLEGE for awhile "hid its light under a bushel" in some dreary-looking premises in Nicholas Street, but was removed hither in the autumn of 1842. In addition to the ordinary details of scholastic training, the students are instructed in various branches of manual labour; they are taught how "to handle the chisel and the saw, the mattock and the spade." They have on the premises a blacksmith's forge,—at which they manufacture all their own implements and tools;—turners' lathes, steam-engines, lithographic presses, power looms, and a host of other appliances, are at the mercy of the "happy family;" and it is wonderful to see to what proficiency these amateur craftsmen attain,—and all, be it remembered, during their intervals of leisure from more important duties. Subordinate in some measure to this "school for school-masters," there is also a Lower School, upon the ground floor, for the children of the poor. Here the incipient masters in turn officiate, and gradually learn, under the superintendence of their worthy chief, the practical duties of their responsible profession. Under the same paternal roof exists another school, more private and commercial in its character and aims, under the special eye and control of the principal, for the sons of the higher and middle classes of society. Of this latter arm it is sufficient to say—

> And higher praise 'twere hard to give,
> Unjust to offer less,—

that it is conducted on the same scale of intelligence and liberality which distinguish the other main branches of the institution.

Some years after the building of the COLLEGE, a Chapel was erected at the south-east corner, for the use of the students; and a chaste little edifice it is, inside as well as out; worthy—if aught here below, indeed, *can* be worthy— of the holy purpose for which it was designed,—the glorious worship of the triune God. The internal fittings and decorations, which are many and beautiful, are almost wholly the work of the industrious students; and, while honourable to their taste in design, reflect the highest credit as well upon their hearts as on their hands.

Beyond, and to the right of the COLLEGE, stands the Cheshire COUNTY LUNATIC ASYLUM; but, this being without the confines of the City, is, by the same token, beyond our pale.

We have now reached the extent of our wanderings northward, for a narrow brook, a short distance away, determines the limits of the city jurisdiction; so, bidding "a long, a last farewell" to the Chester COLLEGE, and to the enchanting prospect its site commands, we will return, nothing loth, to the heart of the city, and to those ravishing chops so anxiously awaiting us at our own hotel.

CHAPTER X.

Llwyd, the Welsh Antiquary.—Chester Fair.—Tennis Court and Theatre.—The Justing Croft.—The Bars.—Steam Mills.—Ragged Schools.—Boughton and St. Paul's Church.—The Spital and George Marsh.—Roman Altar.—St. John Street, and Mechanics' Institution.—Roman Catholic Convent.—St. John's Church and Ruins.—Jacob's Well, and the Anchorite's Cell.—The Groves and the Dee.

WHAT a strange old place this CHESTER of ours is! As we retrace our steps under the NORTHGATE and the WALLS, we seem as if roaming through a city of the middle ages; so oddly does everything around us arrest our attention, and "excite our passing wonder." Those overhanging gables, with darksome pathways burrowed out beneath them, and whose builders were subjects of "Good Queen Bess,"—those two rugged Gateways still marking the course of the old Abbey wall,—the crumbling Abbey itself, more venerable still, and incomparably "richer and rarer" to look upon; these, and yon marvellous Rows, which nobody has ever seen, or ever can see, anywhere but in Chester, afford us ample subjects for contemplation until we arrive at the EASTGATE.

The first street we come to on leaving the Gate is ST. JOHN STREET; but, the good old rule of "first come, first serve," must for once be set aside, since we intend to reserve the locality for the close of the present chapter.

Just opposite to St. John Street, is Bank Place; the house at the top of which was long the residence of Richard Llwyd, the Bard of Snowdon, and the author of "Beaumaris Bay," a zealous, amiable, and intelligent Welsh antiquary. The poet died here in 1835.

Moving away eastward, then, past the end of FRODSHAM STREET, already noticed on our way from the RAILWAY STATION, we discern, upon our left, a long passage, leading up to the COMMERCIAL HALL; and, on the right, a heavy block of buildings, one hundred and sixty feet long by ninety-two feet wide, rejoicing in the name of the UNION HALL. These Halls were erected, the former in 1815, and the latter in 1809, by the Lancashire and Yorkshire merchants, who used formerly to inundate the city with their wares during the continuance of the two great Chester Fairs, in October and July. When first built, these "marts of foreign commerce" were always thronged at the privileged season with both buyers and sellers; but the world is wiser than it was; and even the Cestrians have discovered that one of the worst things they can buy is "a pig in a poke;" and that their own tradesmen sell articles every whit as cheap and as good as did those itinerant pedlars.

Eastgate.

Not far from the Union Hall is the old *Tennis* or *Ball Court*, where Penn the Quaker once preached to his admirers, and which was afterwards occupied as a THEATRE, until the perversion of St. Nicholas' Chapel (now the MUSIC HALL) to the like use. Here the productions of "rare Ben Jonson," and the "immortal Will," together with the minor frivolities of Congreve, Cibber, and Vanbrugh (the latter of whom is claimed as a native of Chester), were doled forth to the patrons of "the legitimate drama." Chester is now destitute of a Theatre; but whether it has suffered materially by the loss, shall be left, so far at least as we are concerned, an open question.

A little farther, upon the left hand, lies QUEEN STREET; its higher or northern portion being anciently known as the *Justing Croft*. Beyond the mere name, history has bequeathed us no record of this spot; but, though England's bard has tritely enough exclaimed—"What's in a name?" there is something in *this* one of more than ordinary significance. It is clear that at one time this was the mimic field on which the youthful chivalry of Chester wielded the lance, battle-axe, and sword; that this was the proud arena where, after their return from the wars of Palestine and of France, the belted knights of Cheshire tried a friendly lance with each other, in the presence of their assembled sweethearts and dames; and here, at "tilt and tourney," met the would-be champions of their county, the Calveleys, the Dones, the Egertons, and the Cholmondeleys, and, mayhap, too, the Grosvenors, the Warburtons, and the Leghs. We could weave—but we won't, for our time is getting short—a page or two of romance about this once favourite haunt. Let us hurry away, then, first casting a glance at two

Chapels in this street—opposition establishments, but near neighbours withal,—the ROMAN CATHOLIC CHAPEL, lately transformed into a Cathedral; and the larger and much handsomer meeting-house of the Calvinists, or INDEPENDENTS.

Once again in Foregate Street, we are soon at the head of LOVE LANE; why so named is a mystery; at all events, its mission of love is now confined to the manufacture of *tobacco-pipes*. At its eastern corner is a handsome house, with spacious area in front, until lately the city residence of the Barnstons of Crewe Hill, a Cheshire family of high lineage and repute. In the area before this house, March 19, 1804, the colours were presented to the *Loyal Cheshire Volunteers*, by the lady of Colonel Barnston, commanding officer of the corps. The house is now converted into the AUCTION MART of the Messrs. Churton, the knock of whose professional hammer vibrates at intervals through its noble rooms.

Onward again past SELLER STREET, and the Octagon Chapel, where the Reverend John Wesley once preached, we are not long arriving at a steep road upon our right hand, called *Dee Lane*, running down to the river side. Near the head of this lane stood an ancient Gateway, stretching right across the main street, bearing the name of THE BARS. From a curious plan of the city in the reign of Elizabeth, this Gateway appears to have had a circular turret on either side; but no trace of these remained at the time of its demolition in 1770. From the Bars extended, to the left and right, the outer line of fortifications which encompassed the city during the period of the SIEGE.

Once clear of the Bars, we have passed into Boughton, having Russell, Steam-Mill, and Stevens Streets, all upon our left hand. STEAM-MILL STREET, anciently *Horn Lane*, derives its present name from the large STEAM CORN-MILLS of Messrs. Frost and Sons, occupying the whole of the northern portion of the street. This is a mammoth establishment, employing a large number of hands, and has been long and successfully carried on by the present proprietors. The premises were destroyed by fire in 1834. Close to these Mills flows the CANAL, on the opposite side of which we have a prospect of another hive of industry, the LEAD WORKS and SHOT TOWER of Messrs. Walker, Parker and Co., already noticed in our earlier rambles.

Returning to the main street, we soon arrive, through "poverty, hunger, and dirt," at *Hoole Lane*, the corner of which is now embellished with a neat little structure, known as the Chester RAGGED SCHOOLS, for the use of those tattered little specimens of humanity ever found about the streets of all populous towns.

The Street widens out at this point, disclosing, upon our left hand, RICHMOND TERRACE, a row of handsome suburban residences with neat gardens in front, overlooking the Dee and the Welsh side of Cheshire,

> A prospect fair, of river, wood, and vale,
> As ever eye could wish for!

The declivity on the right is called *Gallows Hill*, from its being of old time the place where malefactors paid the sad penalty of their misdeeds. But what is this white conventicle-looking edifice which crowns its heights? Surely it is the refuge of some Mormon congregation—the temple, perchance, of some pagan fanaticism? Nay verily, good sirs,—assuage your indignation, for this is a Church of your own communion, a sort of Chapel of Ease to the parish of St. John. The architect was "abroad" when this building was designed; for one less becoming the outward character of a Church it is impossible to conceive. It is dedicated to ST. PAUL, and was opened for divine worship in 1830.

Some twenty or thirty yards farther the road divides in twain—that upon the left being the great highway to Nantwich and London in the days when "*flying* machines" went hence to the metropolis in *a couple of days*!—the disciples of Watt are now ready to convey us thither in six or seven hours! The right-hand road would lead us to Whitchurch and Shrewsbury, if we wanted to go there; but we have not yet done with "rare old Chester." This little plot of land on the right is extra-parochial, forming part of that ancient Hospital for *Lepers*, the ancient lazar-house of St. Giles. In the 'SPITAL, as it is now by corruption called, George Marsh was burnt for his firm adherence to the Protestant faith in the days of Queen Mary; and in the little Cemetery of this Hospital, near which we are standing, his calcined remains now quietly rest "in sure and certain hope."

Beyond this lies the township of GREAT BOUGHTON, and a Chapel, once presided over by the Rev. P. Oliver, a somewhat celebrated nonconformist divine. Near this Chapel, in 1821, a Roman Altar was dug up, in splendid preservation, and about four feet high, bearing the following inscription:—

> NYMPHIS ET FONTIBUS
> LEG. XX. V.V.

the which, being translated, would in English read thus—"To the Nymphs and Fountains, the 20th Legion, the invincible and victorious." So much for BOUGHTON, and its past and present condition; we will now retrace our steps to the head of ST. JOHN STREET.

Moving rapidly down this street, leaving behind us the POST OFFICE, and the entrance to the Blossoms Assembly Room, we pause before a house on our right-hand, approached by a flight of steps, and having a lofty stuccoed front. This is the MECHANICS' INSTITUTION, and is consecrated to the instruction and healthy amusement of that important class of society whose name it bears. In addition to a Library, comprising several thousand volumes, this Institution enjoys the advantages of a News-Room, liberally supplied with the leading daily and weekly papers; together with sundry classes for the special behoof and instruction of the members. During the summer months also, members have the right of free admission to the WATER TOWER MUSEUM, which we described at some length in our "Walk round the Walls." What a marvellous fact it is, that with these benefits within their reach so few mechanics, comparatively, avail themselves of this, *their own* Institution!

Beyond this lie the Schools and minister's house of the Wesleyan Methodists, divided only by a path to the Walls from the WESLEYAN CHAPEL itself. The principles of Wesleyanism found their way into Chester as early as 1760, the first congregation being held at a house in Love Lane. Fifteen years afterwards, the Octagon Chapel in Foregate Street was erected for them, and continued to be their place of worship until the completion of the present edifice in 1811.

But what is there to see within those large folding-doors at the bottom of St. John Street? Are any *Roman remains* to be met with in there? Yes, indeed; but far different, in every point of view, from those we have hitherto been exploring. This is a *noli me tangere* domain; for the elegant mansion and grounds of DEE HOUSE have recently developed, 'neath the double enchantment of money and zeal, into a CONVENT of Nuns. Of the constitution and management of this veiled religious order we are not competent to speak, our sympathies being allied unto quite another creed: but from the specimens we have seen flitting noiselessly about the streets, we may but little expect to hear any of them singing—

> Oh, what a pity such a pretty girl as I
> Should be pent in a Nunnery to weep and to cry.

Let us leave then these recluses to the quiet enjoyment of their lot,— whether it be the nursing of the sick, the feeding of the hungry, or the schooling of the ignorant children of their communion,—and, "pursuing the even tenour of our way," move quickly forward along LITTLE ST. JOHN STREET. The little row of Almshouses erected by Mrs. Salmon in 1738— the premises of Messrs. Royle and Son, builders—and the resuscitated fabric of ST. JOHN'S HOUSE, almost destroyed by fire in the summer of 1855, will each in their turn salute us on our progress, until the eye rests subdued before the silent grandeur of the CHURCH OF ST. JOHN.

ST. JOHN'S is the only Church with any pretensions to antiquity now left to the city outside the Walls,—the minor fanes of St. Thomas, St. John the

Less, and St. Giles, having each disappeared 'neath the hand of the destroyer during the great Civil War. In Roman and early Saxon times the land to the southeast of the city, on both sides the Dee, was most probably a forest—the home of the wild deer, the fox, and the wolf—the genius of civilisation finding ample field for employment within the Walls. In those latter days, Ethelred, son of Penda, being king over Mercia, and withal an amiable and pious prince,

>Myndynge moost the blysse of Heuen,

journeyed towards Chester, on a visit, it may be, to his virgin niece, the holy St. Werburgh, then Abbess of Chester. While there, we are told that, being admonished by God in a vision "to build a Church on the spot where he should find a white hind," the king and his nobles engaged in the chace, and straightway coming upon a white hind at this very place, the royal hunter, in 689, founded and erected the Saxon CHURCH OF ST. JOHN THE BAPTIST. A more beautiful site for the erection of such a Church could scarcely have been chosen. Seated on an eminence overlooking the river Dee,—the rock it rests on washed by a stream of far nobler proportions than the river of *our* day,—its banks studded with primæval woods, above which, and far beyond, the peaks of the Cambrian hills just showed their giant heads,—the yet nearer mountain ranges of Beeston and Peckforton,—the city itself, engirdled by the Walls of their Roman predecessors,—such was the prospect that gladdened the eyes of the good King Ethelred and the chaste Werburga, as they watched the progress of their newly-founded Church.

What were the actual dimensions of the Saxon ST. JOHN'S is now, and must ever remain a mystery;—whether any and what portion of the present edifice may be properly referred back to that remote age is, in like manner, doubtful. There are, however, many who believe, like ourselves, that much of the older work, here and there perceptible, belongs to a period anterior to the Norman conquest. The brothers Lysons, (no mean authority, you'll say) pronounce much of the nave and east end of the church to be late Saxon work—portions, no doubt, of the structure re-edified by Leofric, Earl of Mercia, in 1057. Originally the steeple was in the centre of the Church, at the point where the transept intersects the nave; but in or about 1468, it suddenly gave way, and destroyed in its fall great part of the choir and east end of the Church. This tower was soon after rebuilt, and another erected at the west end of the nave:—the former again fell in 1572, and this time the parishioners declined to restore it. The west steeple shared a similar fate in 1574, destroying the whole of that extremity of the fabric. Look up, from our present position at the Gateway of the Churchyard, and the effects of this mishap will be at once apparent,—the steeple, one hundred and fifty feet high, stands isolated from the main body of the

Church, that portion broken in by the fall having since been suffered to remain so by the authorities of the parish. If we pass round to the west side of the tower, we shall see midway a canopied niche, in which stands the statue of the abbot king Ethelred, caressing at his side the "white hind" of his vision. This statue originally decorated the centre tower; but being found *miraculously unhurt* amongst the heap of rubbish created by that structure in its fall, was removed by the parishioners to its present lofty and dignified position. This steeple enjoys a set of eight peerless bells, by far the most melodious of their kind in the city. Six were cast in 1710, and the other two in 1734, having replaced an older peal, which existed here at least as early as the reign of Henry VII. Doubtless, therefore, during the great Civil War, when the news of a royalist victory reached the ears of the loyal citizens,

> Merrily, merrily rang the bells,
> The bells of St. John's church tower.

And "merrily, merrily" ring they still, as the bridal procession issues from the porch, as well as on days of public rejoicing—whenever, in fact, loyalty, love, or patriotism need their witching strains. So much for the outside of ST. JOHN'S CHURCH,—now for a hasty glance at the interior.

Passing through the "old church porch," adorned with an arch of most beautiful character, the mouldings of which spring from little delicately formed shafts, we enter the sacred edifice at its north-western extremity. Here a prospect awaits us enough to disgust even an out and out Puritan. Hideous galleries of giant build, through which the light of heaven can scarcely find its way,—long rows of high wooden boxes, by those in authority facetiously termed pews!—curtains of green exclusiveness, separating the rich from their brethren the poor—such, alas! are our first impressions of this venerable Church! With such incentives to drowsiness, no wonder the parishioners are so sleepy about their Church, and so painfully apathetic about its much-needed restoration!

Threading our way, so well as we can in the gloom, to the bottom of the centre aisle, we now begin to see, despite these grievous drawbacks, something of the original glory and magnificence of this ancient fabric. Following the line of sight eastward, we feast our eyes on the massive pillars and horse-shoe arches of the Saxon, or it may be early Norman architect:—noble ideas of strength and symmetry had the builder of those days! Above these, the double Triforium of later work stretches along the whole length of the Nave, giving to it an elegance and variety claimed for no other sacred edifice in Cheshire. Originally the Nave was just double its present length, boasting eight of those massive semicircular arches on either side, of which four only now remain,—the other four vanished 'neath the crash of the western steeple.

Having arrived at the east end of the Nave, we find ourselves standing between the four lofty piers which, previous to its demolition, supported the great central tower. At this point the transept divides the nave from the choir, and though shorn of its fair proportions by modern reparations wholly devoid of taste, yet contains enough of the original work to give us an idea of its ancient grandeur. Eastward lay the Choir,—now for the most part in ruins, and shut out from the present Church by an interpolated window of very moderate pretensions. The space beneath this window, once part of the choir, has now become, consequent on these alterations, the Chancel of St. John's.

To the right of the Chancel is another horse-shoe arch of very early work, disclosing, behind, a "fayre chappell," once the burial place of the Warburtons, an ancient Cheshire family. A fine sketch of this Chapel, in his own masterly style, will be found in that now scarce work, Prout's "Antiquities of Chester." The floor is strewed with a number of incised slabs, discovered at various periods in the church or churchyard: three of these have been illustrated by Mr. Boutell, in his valuable works on the history of Christian Monuments. On the opposite side of the Chancel rests a sculptured slab, bearing the recumbent effigy of an ecclesiastic, robed in the chesuble and other priestly vestments of the thirteenth or fourteenth century. The slab, which is somewhat defaced, and without inscription, was found, in December 1855, some feet below the surface, on removing the house on the east side of the porch. This is the third or fourth relic, of a similar character, rescued from destruction by the intelligent zeal of the present rector, the Rev. W. B. Marsden. To the left is the Vestry; and near by, ignominiously stowed away in a corner, lies the crosslegged figure of a warrior, of the twelfth century perhaps, clad wholly in mail, and supposed to represent a redoubtable hero of the Carrington family. Close beside, but totally unconnected with it, lies another incised slab, commemorating one of whom all we know is that inscribed on the stone itself, "HIC JACET JOHENNES LE SERJAUN." Most modern "Guide"-mongers have ignorantly supposed the mailed figure adjoining to be this *Johennes le Serjaun*; but this is an error, for the two relics were dug up in different parts of the churchyard! Numerous other monuments, of more or less interest, lie scattered around; but as we are now arrived at the north chancel door, we will bid adieu to the interior of ST. JOHN'S, and again emerge into the open air.

In the graveyard before us, to the left of what was originally the extreme north of the Transept, stood until the last century an ancient house, called the *Woolstaplers' Hall*, of which all trace has now passed away. Over the churchyard wall we can see the upper portion of the GROSVENOR SCHOOL, a charitable institution, erected and endowed by the first Lord Westminster, but now supported by voluntary contributions. Farther still to the right is the Rectory House, abutting upon Love Street and Barker's Lane, neither of which possesses any charms for us sightseers.

Turning away to the right from the Church door, a few paces will bring us to a decayed and half-ruined wall, in the centre of which is a small pointed arch, known as the entrance-gate to the PRIORY. This arch originally formed part of the *Nunnery of St. Mary*, near the CASTLE, and was placed in its present position on the demolition of the ruins of the former establishment, about thirty years ago. The ground within is, strictly speaking, private; but permission being courteously afforded to visitors, we will quietly step into the interior, and ponder awhile on the scene which now presents itself. The genius of desolation reigns dominant here; this spot, once the holiest of holies, the *sanctum sanctorum* of the Church of St. John, is now a roofless and floorless waste. We are standing on the site of the original choir, whose walls oft resounded with purest melody:—but where *now* are the white-robed train? The occupation of the chorister is gone—the voice of the priest has hence for ever died away, and the hymn of praise, of matin and evensong, no longer echoes along its richly vaulted aisles! Here we see the effects produced by the fall of the centre steeple, in 1470, and again in 1572, laying the whole east end of the structure in ruins. Yet still, amid the general decay, for everything here seems crumbling into dust, the rich old chancel arch (call it Saxon or Norman, whichever you will) maintains erect its venerable crest,—the ivy that clasps it, the trees that overshadow, the mould that corrupts it, serving but to increase and develop its charms. Passing under the arch, we are straightway in the Chancel, and close to the spot where the high altar of ST. JOHN'S of old time stood. Here, it may be, the censor of the priest wafted aloft the incense at the daily sacrifice;—here the anathemas of the church were pronounced against excommunicated sinners;—and yet, here, after a lapse of some four hundred years, rank weeds and grass now desecrate the ground, while the owl and the bat hold their midnight levies in this once "holy place." Cast your eyes o'er that fragment heap, now formed into a sort of rockery,—every stone there, could it but speak, has its tale to tell;—here a shattered niche, there a sepulchral slab, yonder a broken font, there again an image defaced—all rich and glorious in their time, but surrendered now to undeserved decay! Pass we on into one of the chapels, where high up in the wall, snugly housed within the masonry, stands an ancient oak coffin bearing the appropriate inscription of

    Dust to Dust.

St. John's Ruins.

The Priory House was built on the ruins of the priests' houses, but has of itself no other claim to our notice, being little in character with aught else around. Thus, then, have we inspected these venerable ruins, so typical of the vanity of everything human; let us now, all unwilling, tear ourselves away,

> And thence returning, soothly swear,
> Was never scene so sad and fair!

Perhaps the best general idea of the Church and Ruins is obtained from yonder gateway at the east end of the yard, where the eye embraces the whole at one view. During the Siege of Chester, ST. JOHN'S CHURCH was taken and garrisoned by the puritans.

From hence we proceed along a narrow pathway to the right, turning round, as we do so, to take a last fond look at the south side of the Ruins, which, from whatever point viewed, are distinguished alike for their sublimity and beauty. Slightly to the westward, on this side of the Church, stood formerly the *Chapel of St. James*, which the brothers Lysons assert was the original parish church. If this be true, it was probably while St. John's was the Cathedral of the united sees of Lichfield, Coventry, and Chester; in which case *St. James's* must have been even of greater antiquity than the present Church of St. John. There is now no trace existing of this venerable Chapel. Yon block of buildings at the extreme west of the churchyard is known as DEE SIDE, and the two mansions comprising it were erected on the site of the Bishop's Palace and Deanery of the episcopal foundation.

From thence a flight of steps leads down to the GROVES, near a spring of great repute, called JACOB'S WELL; over which is engraved the warning of Christ to the woman of Samaria,

>Whoso drinketh of this water shall thirst again.

Moving along to the eastward, we see a curious old house, crowning the edge of the cliff on the left, and known as the *Anchorite's Cell*. Here it is traditionally affirmed that King Harold, merely wounded, not killed, at the Battle of Hastings, was conveyed by his friends, and lived the life of a hermit for several years. This is an article of faith which you may believe or reject, as the spirit moves you; for ourselves, we are tainted with the leaven of unbelief!

Passing QUEEN'S PARK HOTEL, at the foot of the Suspension Bridge, we see the rich *Grove* of trees which has given to the present locality its name. We are now close to the river side, and feeling, moreover, somewhat tired with our long walk; let us, therefore, with appetites sharpened by exercise, step into the DEVA, a handsome HOTEL overlooking the river, and lay violent siege to its well-stored larder. Take care to lay in a plentiful stock of both liquids and solids ere you quit the Hotel,—and, "would you know the reason why?" Our next chapter will treat us to a "Row on the DEE," and a visit to EATON HALL,—neither of which, as you'll presently see, are feats to be accomplished on an empty stomach!

CHAPTER XI.

The River Dee.—Chester Rowing Club.—The Earl's Eye.—Villas on Dee Banks.—The Water Works.—Eccleston.—Eaton Lodge, and the Iron Bridge.—Eaton Hall.—The Grosvenor Family.—The Belgrave Lodge.—The Interior of the Hall.—Eaton Gardens.—Grosvenor Lodge.

HAVING finished our repast at the DEVA HOTEL, and tested the merits of Huxley's prime ale (we should like to know where you can meet with its equal!), we are now fully charged for a "Row on the DEE." Talk of your Thames and your Tamar, your Tyne and your Clyde! To our minds a quiet little "row up the DEE" has a charm superior far to them all! Yonder gaily-decked barge, adorned with the "red, white, and blue" of old England, is the craft of our choice. While, then, mine host is summoning the oarsmen, and arranging the cushions and seats for our reception, a word or so touching the source of the Dee, and its progress towards Chester, will not be out of place.

Rising in Merionethshire, not far from Dolgelley, a modest little rivulet, fed by a score of tributary brethren, elbows its way through many a chasm and rocky dell, until it reaches BALA LAKE. We have so far been tracing a mere mountain stream; but gathering strength and increased impetuosity as it passes through the centre of this beautiful Lake, our little Welsh brook, twin sister of the Wnion, develops into a River, and henceforward assumes the "local habitation and name" of the DEE. Still, as from its source, a pure Welsh river, the "Druid stream of Deva" gambols cheerily on, through the rich Vale of Corwen, 'neath the frowning ruins of *Castell Dinas Bran*, by the side of the beautiful Abbey of VALLE CRUCIS, and so through LLANGOLLEN, "that sweetest of vales." Winding its way thence, through Overton and Bangor,—the latter the scene of the massacre of the British monks,—our river proceeds by a series of zigzags on its course towards HOLT; before reaching which, it serves as the boundary line between Denbighshire and Cheshire. On the Welsh side of the river stand the town and castle of HOLT, an important post in the Anglo-Welsh wars. On the opposite side is FARNDON, connected with Holt by an ancient stone bridge; and from this, the DEE passes ALDFORD and EATON on its way to CHESTER and the Irish Sea.

River Dee, and Groves

But see; "our bark is by the shore," and the boatmen are awaiting us; let us, then, take our seats beneath its awning, and launching out into the stream, cast a momentary glance at the landscape behind us. In the foreground is the DEVA, "our marine Hotel," half hidden from view by yon rich Grove of trees stretching along the river's edge. Behind, and far above it, the tower of ST. JOHN'S CHURCH proudly shows its rugged form. To the left is the Queen's Park Suspension Bridge, more particularly noticed in our "Walk round the Walls." Away under the Bridge we can see a small portion of the WALLS near the Wishing Steps; and beyond that, again, the DEE MILLS and BRIDGE, of ancient fame. Talking of the Dee Mills, of course you know the song, the rare old song, of the "Miller of the Dee,"—that "miller hale and bold," the burden of whose song

> For ever used to be,—
> I envy nobody, no, not I!
> And nobody envies me!

How few millers there are, who can say as much nowadays!

At length we are off, at a stately pace, for "steady's the word," in a Chester barge, and soon we leave the GROVES and the Queen's Park Villas behind us in the distance. Having rounded Aikman's Gardens, we are opposite the grounds of the ROYAL CHESTER ROWING CLUB. We take a pride in our rowing, we citizens of Chester,—and not without reason, for in 1855, our "crack crew" were twice victors at the Henley Regatta, and then and there acknowledged "Champions of the Isis and the Thames!" Whew! there go the "Royals"—the champion crew, old Chester's pride!—at a spanking pace, which nought but sterling metal could possibly maintain! They are out for their daily exercise, under the care of their trainer; the smile on whose face betokens the delight with which he views their performance. They are bad ones to beat, are those amateurs of Chester!

Here is *Billy Hobby's Field*, with its Well of pure water, bearing the same obscure but euphonious name. The meadows on our right were anciently known as the *Earl's Eye*, and used to be covered with water at every tide. A few more strokes of the oar, and we are scudding it past a second grove of trees, overshadowing the river for a considerable distance. The DEE here forms a magnificent crescent, its left bank studded with handsome villas,— foremost among which, "embosomed in foliage," stands DEE HILLS, the residence of Mr. Titherington; while, farther on, we see the new and elegant range of villas, recently erected by that gentleman, called SANDOWNE TERRACE. To these succeed Richmond Villas, and Barrelwell, the sloping gardens of which form a pleasing object in the landscape.

We are now speeding along in front of the WATER WORKS, an establishment which has literally worn itself out in "the temperance cause," and now, in a great measure, superseded by the New Works lately erected in higher Boughton. Just above is ST. PAUL'S CHURCH, of which we told you enough in our last chapter.

Onward again, past West Mount and Dee Banks, we are soon in front of another range of villas, of recent construction, called DEE VIEW, from the long stretch of the Dee which the site commands. This part of the River takes the name of the *Long Reach*, until we come to IRON BRIDGE, vulgarly *Heron Bridge*,—yonder house amid the trees—the pleasant residence of C. W. Potts, Esq.

Yonder is the tower of ECCLESTON CHURCH; and as we are now nearing the village, we may land, if we choose, and indulge in a hasty stroll of inspection. ECCLESTON is the pet village, and wholly the property of the Marquis of Westminster, whose elegant mansion, EATON HALL, we are so soon about to visit. Every house in this village is a picture of itself, clothed in woodbine and choicest evergreen, and adorned with small, but sweetly smelling gardens. The CHURCH is a modern structure of red sandstone, having taken the place of an older temple in 1810. The interior has recently been altered and re-decorated by Lord Westminster, and is now a pretty little model of a village sanctuary. The space above the altar is occupied by Westall's grand painting, "Joseph of Arimathea begging the Body of Jesus from Pilate."

It is now time to retrace our steps, and row glibly on towards the IRON BRIDGE and LODGE, the former erected, in 1824, by the late Lord Westminster, at a cost of 8000*l*. Another course, and one we ourselves prefer, is to row merely to the EATON LODGE, a short distance up the river, and there, leaving our friendly barge, take the road along the Park,

> 'Twixt avenues of proud ancestral trees,

till we find ourselves suddenly close to the western entrance to EATON HALL, the princely seat of the MARQUIS OF WESTMINSTER.

It is no part of our present business to assume the herald's place, by painting the genealogy of the noble house of GROSVENOR; else might we show that the family trace back, in the direct male line, to the Norman Conquest,—how that Gilbert le *Grosveneur* (or the *Great Hunter*), nephew of Hugh Lupus, first Norman Earl of Chester, came over with his uncle in the train of King William,—that Robert le Grosvenor, a "red-cross knight," fought with much distinction under Richard I. in the great Crusade,—how that another Robert covered himself with honour at the battle of Cresy,—that his grandson Robert was defendant in the famous "Scroope and Grosvenor suit," concerning the ancient arms of those two great families. All this we could show,—and that later still, in the Great Rebellion, when other magnates joined the traitorous band, the "House of Eaton" remained steadfast in its loyalty, and, in the person of Sir Richard Grosvenor and his son Roger, raised the *posse comitatus* of Cheshire, and gallantly therewith did battle for the King. But we must forbear,—for see, we are now approaching the entrance porch at the West Front of the HALL.

The EATON estate passed to the GROSVENORS in the fifteenth century, by the marriage of Raufe le Grosvenor with Joan, daughter of John de Eaton; previously to which, for two centuries, the family had been settled at Hulme, near Northwich.

A mansion of considerable importance existed here long prior to the seventeenth century, being then usually known as EATON BOAT, from its proximity to the ancient ferry of that name, across the river Dee. Sir Thomas Grosvenor, however, son and grandson of the two ardent royalists already mentioned, took unto himself a wife, in the person of Mary Davies, of Ebury, county Middlesex; through whom he acquired her father's valuable estates in Westminster. The lady, it would seem, admired not the humble palace at EATON BOAT; for Sir Thomas soon after erected in its stead a nobler mansion, from designs furnished by Sir John Vanbrugh, the celebrated architect and dramatist, who is confidently affirmed to have been a native of Chester. This Hall, which was of brick, with a heavy lanthorn roof, was pulled down, in 1803, by the late Lord Westminster, who at once set to work with the magnificent fabric we see now before us. It is built of white freestone from the Manley quarry; Porden being the architect originally consulted. Nine tedious years and a mint of money were exhausted in its erection; and in 1823–5, two new wings were added, so as almost to double its original length. Critics now began to complain that its height was wholly dis-proportioned to its length, and impertinent scribes picked all manner of holes even in the architecture itself.

These and other considerations moved the present worthy Marquis, in 1845, to attempt the remedying of these defects. With his accustomed sagacity, he called in the professional aid of Mr. Burn, an eminent London architect, to whose ability and judgment his lordship confidently entrusted the work. How that gentleman fulfilled his mission it skills not for us to declare,—let the edifice before us speak for itself. Erected and adorned regardless of expense, tasteful and grand in design and execution, this princely pile, Gothic in every material characteristic, is a model of all that is rich and elegant in domestic architecture. Look up for a moment at the gracefully light yet massive structure,—at its sculptured niches, its crocketted pinnacles and embattled parapets, its windows filled with gorgeous tracery, every available space upon its surface bristling with shields charged with the heraldic crests and quarterings of the Grosvenor family,—and say if the sight, rich even to profusion, and wholly indescribable, savours not more of a palace of fairy land than of the house and home of a retiring English nobleman! The HALL itself exceeds four hundred and fifty feet in length; but in addition to that we have the Stables and outbuildings continuing the line, in the same Gothic style, their centre crowned with a lofty Clock Turret of chaste design. The entire length of the Hall and offices is nearly seven hundred feet. But we must not any longer linger here, for it is high time we were turning our attention to the interior of the HALL.

Mounting the flight of steps under the porch,—from the top of which, through that dark vista of trees just a mile in length, we see the BELGRAVE LODGE,—we present our tickets of admission to the attendants, and are forthwith ushered into the ENTRANCE HALL of certainly the most magnificent mansion in Britain. This is an apartment eminently calculated to prepare the visitor for the gorgeous splendour everywhere pervading this far-famed Hall. In height it extends to two stories of the house, the floor being composed of the most richly varied tesselated marbles of the utmost rarity. Imagine a floor, less than forty feet square, costing its noble owner sixteen hundred guineas! Glance up at the chaste and elegant groined ceiling, the intersections relieved with foliated bosses and heraldic devices,—foremost among the latter being the arms of the Grosvenors, "azure, a garb or," confirmed to the family after their bootless legal suit with the Scroopes. From the centre of the ceiling depends a gorgeous brass chandelier lamp, of exquisite workmanship. Opposite the entrance runs a Gothic screen of most elaborate character, supporting and half hiding an open gallery, which leads from the upper apartments on the north to those on the south side of the Hall. This screen is furthermore decorated with fourteen heraldic coats, in high relief, representing some of the numerous quarterings of the Grosvenor family. On the right and left are two chaste and beautiful white marble chimney-pieces, corresponding in design with the rest of the apartment. Above these, and on either side, are rich canopied niches, eight in number, in which are placed stalwart figures of warriors, clad in belted mail, and other ancient armour. In the lower recesses of the screen are two massive vases and pedestals of Peterhead marble. Four marble statues give a finishing grace to this noble ENTRANCE HALL,—that on the right representing "Telemachus Arming," by Bienaimé; opposite to it, on the left, being Rinaldi's classic group, "Ulysses Recognised by his Dog." The other two present to us Gibson's conception of "The Wounded Amazon," and the equally meritorious "Dying Amazon," by Wolff.

From the ENTRANCE HALL we pass through the Gothic arch upon the left, along the GREAT CORRIDOR,—a handsome gallery, near five hundred feet in length, enriched with numerous portraits of the Grosvenor family, as well as a recumbent statue, in marble, of a *Sleeping Bacchante*,—to the private or DOMESTIC CHAPEL of the mansion. This is reached by a short gallery to the left, the two gothic windows of which are adorned with medallions of *The Resurrection* and the *Madonna*, in richly stained glass. The CHAPEL, which measures about 40 × 30 feet, has a handsome groined roof, tastefully relieved with floriated bosses and circular finials, adorned with sacred monograms and other devices. The light of day shines into the Chapel through three rich pointed windows, upon the west side, each filled with stained glass of pristine beauty. In the centres of these we see eighteen vesica-shaped medallions, depicting scenes and events in the life of Our Blessed Lord, viz., in the left-hand window,—"The Annunciation," "The Virgin and Child," "The Wise Men of the East," "The Shepherds Watching," "The Presentation in the Temple," and "The Flight into Egypt." In the right-hand window we have—"Christ giving Sight to the Blind," "Blessing Little Children," "Raising the Dead Lazarus," "The Woman of Samaria," "The Baptism of Christ," and "Christ Walking on the Sea." The subjects in the centre window are—"The Last Supper," "The Agony in the Garden," "Christ bearing His Cross," "The Angel declaring the Resurrection," "Christ appearing to Mary," and "The Ascension." Contrary to usual ecclesiastical rule, the reading-desk and communion-table, of carved oak, are at the south end of the Chapel. Near by is the stall of the noble Marquis, which, together with the rest of the seats, is of oak, appropriately carved, under the superintendence of Mr. Morison, then clerk of the works, but now permanently employed by Lord Westminster in a higher capacity. On the north wall formerly hung the painting now decorating the east side, representing "St. Michael's Contest with the Dragon," a copy by Evans from the original by Guido. A handsome window has recently been introduced into the north wall, and filled with embossed fleur-de-lys quarries of plate-glass, producing an admirable effect. Over the communion-table we perceive Weiser's spirited copy of Rubens' "Descent from the Cross." The servants' entrance is by another door upon the left, leading away to their apartments on the basement story.

Leaving the Chapel by the door at which we entered, we repass through the lobby, observing in our course the fine bust of Our Saviour, in marble, upon our right-hand. Thence crossing the Great Corridor, we move along, through a short passage, into the DINING-ROOM. This is a splendid apartment, chastely beautiful in all its details, and though less profusely gorgeous than some of its companions, is yet sufficiently so to justify its position as the great Banqueting Room of the mansion. The ceiling is a combination of rich and delicate tracery, dotted here and there with the coats armorial of the family, and radiating almost imperceptibly towards the centre, whence depends, from its elaborate boss, a massive chandelier. Three richly-carved mahogany sideboards, and a splendid mirror in five Gothic panels, add a grace to this room, the walls of which are caparisoned in maroon and gold on a white ground. Each corner of the room has a chaste canopied niche, adorned with statuary from the studio of Sir R. Westmacott,—those at the north end representing the Crusader, "Sir Robert le Grosvenor," in mail armour, and "Mary, Lady Grosvenor," the heiress of Westminster. At the south end we have "Sir Gilbert le Grosvenor," the Norman patriarch of the family, and "Joan de Eaton," afterwards Lady Grosvenor, a chaste and graceful conception of the sculptor. Over the rich marble fireplace is an original *chef-d'œuvre*, of Rubens—"The Meeting of David and Abigail,"—on either side of which are full-length portraits of the first Marquis and Marchioness of Westminster, painted by Jackson.

From this Room we pass through a handsome doorway into the ANTE-DINING-ROOM, a smaller and much plainer apartment, the walls painted a beautiful arabesque of white and gold on a green ground, producing an extremely rich and pleasing effect. The inlaid oak-floor, the delicate ceiling, and the stained glass portraits of three of the Norman Earls of Chester, which ornament the windows, all merit our attention; but we must hurry away, and by a doorway opposite, pass into the SALOON.

This apartment is stated, and with every good reason, to be without exception the most elegant room in Great Britain! Let other scribes presume, if they will, to attempt a description of this sumptuous hall of state,—*we*, for our part, shrink dismayed from the task. To do anything like justice to its manifold merits would require far more time, and infinitely greater powers, than *we* have at command; let us be content, then, shortly and without parade, to point out a few of its prevailing features. Measuring nearly eleven yards square, the graceful arches intersecting the angles invest it with quite an octagonal appearance. From these, and the walls, springs the roof, with its majestic dome of dazzling splendour—a matchless epitome of all that is rich, chaste, and beautiful in decorative art. The prevailing colours are crimson, blue, and gold, and these so judiciously blended that the eye never tires in its fascinating mission; but still gazing upwards, allured and bewildered, finds new beauties and richer charms, the longer one remains in this wondrous SALOON. From the marble base springs a lofty fretwork of painted mosaic, in close imitation of the Ambassador's Court in the Alhambra Palace,—that peerless relic of old Moorish magnificence. Higher still range panels and medallions, apparently in high relief; but this curious effect is a mere illusion of the painter, for the whole of the walls are perfectly flat. Five handsome landscapes, also painted on the walls, adorn this Saloon, four being the work of Mr. Telbin, of London,—and the fifth the production of Mr. John Morris, of Chester, to whose talented management the entire decorative arrangements were confided. The imitation basso-relievos over the doors are the work of a humble but talented artist, the late William Tasker, of Chester. The windows of the Saloon are in perfect consonance with the apartment itself, and contain six handsome figures, representing "William the Conqueror" and his uncle "Odo, Bishop of Bayeux;" "Sir Gilbert le Grosvenor," nephew of King William, and an imaginary portrait of his wife; "Sir Robert le Grosvenor" (of Scroope and Grosvenor notoriety); and "Joan Pulford," his wife. The view from these windows, which open out to the TERRACE and cloistered arcade on the East side of the Hall, is one of rich and varied beauty. In the foreground we see the elegant TERRACE, GARDENS, and LAKE; and just beyond, catch here and there a glimpse of the "tortuous Dee." Between yon avenue of trees, and some sixteen miles away, the landscape ends with the towering, rain-clad hill of Beeston, and the noble baronial Castle of Peckforton. Our woodcut illustration of the HALL is taken from near the Terrace beneath us, which is perhaps the best point for viewing to perfection this side of the mansion. Turning again to the Saloon, our eyes rest on the massive and elegant folding door of carved oak, which, thrown open, reveals to us the great ENTRANCE HALL. These two apartments, thus seen at one view, for gorgeous magnificence, stand alone and unrivalled.

Eaton Hall, East Front.

We now pass on, by the south door of the Saloon, into the ANTE-DRAWING-ROOM, differing materially in its enrichment from the room we have just quitted, but withal an apartment of chastened beauty. It has a flat ceiling, adorned with delicate tracery in cream-colour and gold; the walls painted a rich arabesque, enchased throughout with red and green on a cream-coloured ground. Three bookcases, filled with modern 'light reading' in elegant bindings, add a grace to the apartment,—the fine windows of which contain stained glass figures of Hugh Cyvelioc, Randle Blondeville, and John Scot, the last of the line of Norman Earls of Chester.

Next we have the DRAWING-ROOM, second only to the Saloon in the splendour of its decorations. Fifty feet in length—its ceiling sparkling with heraldic shields, and honeycombed with tracery in cream-colour and gold—its walls hung with rich crimson silk damask; its superb niches, vases, and chandelier; its marble chimney-piece and mirror; its glorious original pictures of the "Wise Men's Offering," by Rubens, the "Battles of the Boyne and La Hogue," by West, and other celebrated works of art,—all invest this room with a halo which no words of ours can possibly do justice to. It must be seen to be appreciated; and to be admired as it deserves, must be closely scrutinised in all its bearings.

From the Drawing-Room we proceed, along the corridor, into the LIBRARY, a spacious apartment at the southern extremity of the HALL. This well-proportioned room measures sixty-two feet by fifty feet; a range of pillars on either side adding symmetry and strength to its richly groined ceiling. Three bold Gothic windows, facing south, east, and west, shed a fine flood of light into the room; the oaken bookcases of which are filled to overflowing with the richest and rarest works of ancient and modern literature. Upon the left we observe a fine organ, in a carved mahogany case. But the most attractive objects, apart from the library itself, are the remarkably chaste and beautiful conceptions in marble of "Cephalus and Procris," by Rinaldi, which occupies the centre, and the quite as enchanting *chefs-d'œuvres* of Wyatt—"Glycera" and "Hebe." In this room also is preserved one of those extremely rare Romano-British ornaments, a golden TORQUE, discovered some years ago near Caerwys, in Flintshire. The Torque was an ornament worn round the necks of illustrious British warriors: Queen Boadicea, and Llewellyn, Lord of Yale, are both recorded to have been so decorated. Who was the original owner of the one now before us is a matter, of course, wrapped in impenetrable obscurity.

But time presses, and we, too, must press on. Passing out from the Library, we may now direct our steps to the STATE BEDROOM. This is a plain, yet elegant, apartment,—its prime feature being the mahogany State Bed, most elaborately carved, whereon have reposed the sleeping majesty of England, and other royal and distinguished personages. The handsome mirror, the rich green Brussels carpet, and other furniture of the chamber, are all in chaste and admirable keeping with the principal Bedroom of this "Palace on the Dee."

Turn we now to the GRAND STAIRCASE, a portion of the Hall which may vie with any we have yet visited, whether for beauty or variety. A flight of stairs running up from the centre, continued again towards the right and left, conduct to the second gallery, and to the private apartments on the higher story. Opposite to us, on either side as we ascend, are two Egyptian statues in coloured marble, within rich Gothic niches. The decorations of this staircase are sumptuous in the extreme, blue and gold being the predominant colours,—the whole producing to the eye of taste a grand, impressive, and lasting effect. Among the paintings embellishing this staircase and its vicinity are the "Leicestershire Hunt," by Ferneley, the "Grosvenor Hunt," by Stubbs, and another of the "Cheshire Hunt," all three introducing portraits of the Grosvenor family, either of the last or present generation. Another picture deserving our notice is that of a "Brood Mare and Foals," painted also by Stubbs. The private Sitting-Rooms of Lord and Lady Westminster, which with other apartments adjoin the GREAT CORRIDOR, are not exhibited to strangers. Numerous pieces of statuary, family portraits, and racing pictures, many of them of great interest, arrest our attention as we move along the Corridor; but having now returned to the ENTRANCE HALL, we must beat a hasty retreat from this scene of enchantment, and, emerging from its portals, bid "a last, a long farewell" to EATON HALL, the palatial home of the Marquis of Westminster.

Before we do so, however, if provided beforehand with tickets from "our publisher," we may take a turn round the spacious GARDENS on the east side of the Hall. Though time and space alike forbid us to enlarge upon their charms, the GARDENS of EATON will amply repay the careful inspection of every admirer of "nature, art-adorned." The rich groves of trees—the rare shrubs and flowers, with their attendant perfumes—the crystal conservatory—the massive statuary—the dolphin fountain—the Roman altar, dedicated by the Twentieth Legion to the "Nymphs and Fountains"—the fairy lake—the verdant lawns, and walks of "sweet umbrageous beauty,"—each and all combine to invest these GARDENS with a charm peculiarly their own! Gladly would we linger all day in this sylvan retreat,—but we must away!—and exchanging our barge for a cab with a party just arrived (cabman and boatmen first of all consenting), we are soon out of sight of the "Palace on the DEE."

Moving rapidly along the avenue, past yon herd of timid deer, startled into flight at our approach, we soon flit beneath the archway of a lodge which marks the boundary of the park. A ride of two miles, through a serpentine avenue of "old hereditary trees," now remains to us; and from this we emerge only to behold the GROSVENOR GATEWAY, with old CHESTER in the distance "lending enchantment to the view!" The GROSVENOR GATEWAY was erected in 1838, on the site of Overleigh Hall, once the manorial seat of the Cowpers of Overleigh. This lodge is a copy of St. Augustine's Gate, at Canterbury, altered (some say improved) here and there by Mr. Jones, architect of Chester. Built, like the Hall itself, of white freestone, enriched with a profuseness of carving and heraldic sculpture, this ENTRANCE LODGE to the EATON Estate forms a fitting introduction to the magnificent mansion we have just quitted, and of which, in conclusion, we may truly enough say that

> Take it for all in all,
> We ne'er shall look upon its like again!

In five minutes more our cab is rolling over the well-paved streets of CHESTER. And now, as you are off by the next train, and as the best of friends must part, we will shake you by the hand, and trusting you have enjoyed yourselves under our protection, wish you, with all our heart, a swift and pleasant journey to your HOME, SWEET HOME!

In closing this account of EATON HALL, it is our pleasing duty gratefully to acknowledge Lord Westminster's kindness and favour, not only in throwing open the mansion and grounds to us on a "private day," but also in affording us every possible assistance in our humble endeavours, however feebly, to do justice to his peerless Cheshire home.

To G. Allen, Esq., his Lordship's house steward, as well as to Mr. J. Morison, we are especially beholden,—to the former, for his courteous attention in pointing out every prominent feature of the Hall—and to the latter, for numerous architectural and other data, of essential service to us in our "labour of love."

VISITORS are reminded that EATON HALL AND GROUNDS are, by the kindness of Lord Westminster, exhibited to the public during the months of JUNE, JULY, and AUGUST, subject to the following judicious regulations:—

> On Mondays, Tuesdays, and Wednesdays, between the hours of ten and four, to Residents and Tourists generally; and on Thursdays also, during the same hours, to *Foreigners only*, or *Travellers from a distance*. In order to do away with the unsatisfactory principle of giving fees to the servants, his Lordship has authorised the sale of ADMISSION TICKETS, in accordance with the following tariff. The money realised by the sale of these Tickets is generously appropriated by Lord Westminster to the benefit of the funds of the various CHESTER CHARITIES.

TICKETS		
	s.	*d.*
To admit one person to the HOUSE *only*	2	0
,, three ,,	5	0
,, five ,,	7	6
To admit one person to the GARDENS *only*	1	6
,, three ,,	3	0
,, five ,,	5	0

Without such TICKETS (which may be obtained in Chester from "Our Publisher," MR. T. CATHERALL, EASTGATE ROW, Messrs. Prichard and Roberts, or from the ROYAL and ALBION HOTELS) no persons will, on any account, be admitted into the HALL.

EATON HALL being distant nearly four miles from Chester, CABS, &c. can be obtained either on the STAND in Eastgate Street,—from the principal Hotels,—or from Mr. T. Griffith, cab proprietor, Nicholas Street.

FOR the convenience of those Visitors who have no faith in human nature, especially when hidden under the "thick skin of a cabman," we have appended a list of

CAB FARES IN CHESTER.

Not exceeding three persons: to or from the Railway Station in Brook Street—from or to any part of the city, within the point where the Whitchurch and Northwich roads turn off—Abbot's Grange and the College—the Sluice House, including Crane Street and Paradise Row—the May-pole in Handbridge, and the New Bridge Toll-house, *One Shilling.*

The same distance: *four* persons, *One Shilling and Sixpence.* Any distance beyond the Borough, *One Shilling* per mile.

No gratuities to be demanded by the drivers of any cars plying within the borough, and no charge for luggage not exceeding 100 lbs. in weight.

FARES TO OR FROM ANY OTHER PART OF THE CITY.

Not exceeding three persons: any distance not exceeding one mile, *One Shilling*; and at the rate of *One Shilling* per mile for every additional mile; and *Sixpence* for every additional half-mile or fractional part of half-a-mile.

For *four* persons: any distance not exceeding one mile, *One Shilling and Sixpence*; any distance exceeding one mile, and not exceeding two miles, *Two Shillings*; any distance exceeding two miles, at the rate of *Two Shillings* for the first mile, and *One Shilling* per mile for every additional mile, and *Sixpence* for every additional half-mile or fractional part of half-a-mile.

BY TIME.

Not exceeding one hour, *Two Shillings and Sixpence*; and *Sixpence* for every fifteen minutes and fractional part of fifteen minutes beyond the hour. In all cases it shall be at the option of the driver to charge by time or distance.

Milton Keynes UK
Ingram Content Group UK Ltd.
UKHW030909151124
451262UK00006B/864